STYLES OF LIVING

The best of **CASA**
VOGUE

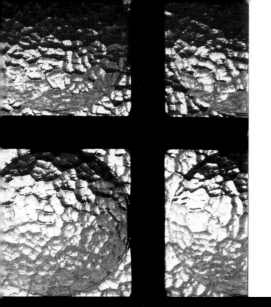

ISA VERCELLONI

STYLES OF LIVING

The best of CASA VOGUE

306 color illustrations

RIZZOLI
NEW YORK

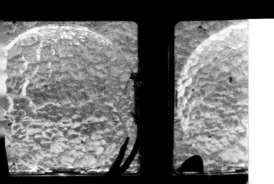

ACKNOWLEDGMENTS

I want to take this opportunity of thanking all those who have helped me in the work of documenting and describing so many different ways of living during the sixteen years that I have been editing Casa Vogue: the architects, photographers, my editorial staff and the magazine's many contributors.

In particular, I would like to mention Marina Rovera, Giovanni Odoni, Maria Vittoria Carloni, Enrichetta Ritter, Giovanna Ralli as well as Giuliana Corsini, Maddalena Sisto, Aldolfo Natalini, Rainer Krause, Barbara Radice, Matteo Thun, Bepi Maggiori, Valerio Morpurgo, Gianni Perotti, Paolo Rinaldi, Adriana Monti, Donatella Smetana, Miloska Pavesi and Laura Maggi, because without their collaboration it would not have been possible for me to have completed this book.

First published in the United States
of America in 1985 by
RIZZOLI INTERNATIONAL PUBLICATIONS, INC.
597 Fifth Avenue, New York, NY 10017

Library of Congress Cataloging in Publication Data
Main entry under title:

Styles of living.

1. Architecture, Domestic—Italy—Themes, motives.
2. Architecture, Domestic—Italy—Conservation and restoration. 3. Interior decoration—Italy—History—20th century—Themes, motives. I. Vercelloni, Isa. II. Casa vogue.
NA7355.S7 1985   728   84-43109
ISBN 0-8478-0598-0

Printed and bound in Great Britain

CONTENTS

INTRODUCTION

After fifteen years as editor (since 1968, when the first number came out), I still can't really say what for me constitutes the best of *Casa Vogue*. Perhaps the best is summed up in the magazine's basic formula, the free-ranging eclecticism which at the time so flouted all the rules of specialist publishing – and which has been so widely imitated since. In the editorial of that first number, I wrote:

'Each new era – and one begins every day – requires a new style. Not a day passes therefore without the pulse-takers – the marketing men and observers of the social scene – announcing that in the field of interior design, as in every other field, one fashion is finished and we must rush to be among the first to latch on to the next. "Colour is old-hat, everything's black and white now." "White has had its day, now we're all for neutral tints." "Inflatable furniture's out, long live the transparent look." "Away with Art Nouveau and Art Déco, this year everyone's going back to early Futurism." Fortunately, today, we are liberating ourselves increasingly from fashion, stepping aside from fashion in the old sense of the term. No mandarin of taste can wake up one fine morning and impose his or her *diktat* on the world expecting it to be accepted. In this climate, ideas are worth more than styles, and each of us is free to seek out the beautiful, or at least the attractive, wherever we please, and to create it by the means best suited to us. Eclecticism, in this sense, is not a compromise but a conquest, and in each case involves a choice both more hazardous and more interesting than any homogeneous solution. *Casa Vogue*, besides giving ample coverage to the most important new trends in Italian interior decorating and furniture design, will show examples from all over the world of *lived-in* houses, where the taste, preferences and personality of the owners will count for more than the architect or designer.'

Over 150 numbers have come out since then, and the magazine has always stayed true to that course. Still, I am not really sure if that is the best of *Casa Vogue*.

Perhaps the best has been provided by certain famous photographers, with the 'added value' their pictures have given to our texts. Perhaps certain features on avant-garde architecture. Or certain very subtle, delicate still-lifes devotedly created in the studio by Aldo Ballo, putting together different articles of design in such a manner that the whole can light a new path, point a fresh trend. Or the best can most likely be found in certain other pictures which discover and bring out, through the photographic object, unexpected associations between art, architecture and design, and sometimes fashion: hidden parallels between various expressive currents, which may escape the eye of the ordinary observer but are easier to discern from the privileged viewpoint of a magazine's editorial office.

Or perhaps the best can be seen in certain features on curious, bizarre ways of living, utterly remote from our own everyday experience. But, in selecting the best from these, how is one to equate the houseboats of Kashmir with the mud skyscrapers of the Yemen, or the house which some person has filled with nothing but bicycles, or the one with a newspaper kiosk planted slap in the centre? What I can say is that, while Chareau's 'Maison de Verre' in Paris remains the best example of interior architecture to have crossed our pages in all these years, the piece of architecture I *love* the most is the 'Teatro del Mondo', Aldo Rossi's little floating theatre, at the same time so fragile and definitive, improbable and true, ephemeral and timeless, poetic and absolute; and so fascinating, fabulously navigating the waters of the Venetian Lagoon. . . . However, in the end, it seemed best to return to the theme which is the *raison d'être* of the magazine: that of places for living in. In this book, you will find gathered together some of the most beautiful, interesting, prestigious, significant or amusing homes reproduced in *Casa Vogue*.

You will find works by the biggest international names, the most talented architects. Many of these have become – some already were – my best friends. This in itself would be of no interest, except that they have also become the best friends of *Casa Vogue*. And in fact it is thanks to them and their assistance that the magazine has been able to explore new directions, striving always to stay on the crest of the wave, alerting readers to all the new ferments, drifts, trends, in the fields of furnishing, architecture, the visual image, long before these have been taken up and entered the domain of mass consumption.

Maybe this is the best aspect of magazine journalism: that superbly intricate network (which continues to grow and link up with other networks and only in certain places and times gets overstretched and starts to reveal gaps), a network of relationships based on mutual understanding, on collaboration, on exchange of information, on a more or less spontaneous affinity, on predilections, recommendations, discoveries – and sometimes on gut enthusiasms, on sudden shared passions – a network that establishes itself between the information media and the artistic and cultural operators, the creative artists, the photographers, architects, designers from all over the world. It is this that determines the shape of a magazine and gradually aligns it to the changing course of events; it is this, I believe, that our more assiduous readers perceive and appreciate.

A challenge for those producing a magazine such as ours in the growing of antennae sufficiently sensitive to pick up all incoming messages, including those arriving from afar, and above all those which, being aimed at the future, seem to travel at a greater altitude; which means these antennae of ours must also grow pretty tall.

Our network may be intricate but must not be indiscriminate, because we must not pick up the dross: the banalities, the repetitions, the mannerisms; the tedious and presumptuous; the *déjà vu*, the dust-collectors, the *de trop*;

the forced or shrill. Above all, we must avoid *perbenismo* – that castrating excess of good taste which can stifle any attempt at authentic innovation and originality. All these must be discarded.

Every now and then someone, with the best intention of helping us in our quest for new material, asks me: but what does a home have to have to be chosen for publication in *Casa Vogue?* The answer is very elusive, because no single recipe exists. Usually I reply: I look at all the homes we have featured to date, all very different from each other, and try to discover one tiny common denominator. If you find one, forget it – and put something else in its place, something new. The world is moving on and, to keep up, magazines are having to run just that bit further. It doesn't matter if the novelty is ephemeral or a bit mad. So much the better. A young Middle Eastern prince who makes a hobby of interior design says one of the reasons he buys *Casa Vogue* is that each time he opens a new number it is like being struck by *une bouffée de délire* – a gust of delirium.

Choosing houses to put in a book is not quite the same thing. A magazine article, however exciting, may be a passing fancy; a book is for living with. So one starts to look for homes that have something more than novelty to commend them: homes with a charm that is timeless, or homes that so perfectly reflect the time when they were conceived and built that they will ever be tangible witnesses to their time and place, records of a culture and lifestyle perhaps irrecoverable but – in its day – valid and meaningful.

As always, and as for every other thing – human beings included – the charm of a house consists first and foremost of its mysterious alchemy of associations, the delicate balance – and at times imbalance – of associations: associations between the house and its creator, between the house and those who live in it; between the house, with its surroundings space, and the town or countryside which contains it (between nature and culture); between its transmission of expressive charge and the silence and quiet it can offer its occupants (between what it says and what it keeps to itself); associations of space, light and colour; associations between old and new, between references and allusions, between memories and expectations (between past and future). Associations between keeping the world out and letting the present in. Also associations between materials, technologies and functions on the one side and forms and ideas on the other – but that is an old story, and we are exploring something more imponderable and subtle than that. In regard to functions, it is better for a house not to be too specific but to keep its options open: in practice, I believe that a good house should cater for all life's unforeseeable eventualities.

Once upon a time the house was a place to which we entrusted our memories, the most personal part of ourselves, the most lasting, destined even to be passed down from generation to generation. The family house rarely changed: it remained always the same, faithful and occasionally awkward, like certain elderly servants who know us too well to swallow our foibles. Today, by contrast, people don't want such maternal, protective houses, or not just those. They want transitory houses, halting places on a voyage whose end they cannot foresee: young, self-reliant houses, without problems, houses that know how to endure infidelity and neglect without bitterness. If that contributes to a freer, happier and less inhibited lifestyle ... so be it. If the desire for simple, clean, uncluttered things lead to a simpler, cleaner, less cluttered life ... that's fine too. But what if it is also due to a paucity of invention, a cramped imagination? What then? Then we see instantly that simplicity turns to squalor. 'Mais la chose qui ose', as Marcel Duchamp would say, should be to feel a free citizen in your home while still giving free rein to fantasy and imagination. One should never forget that the inessential is indispensable. As Robert Bresson maintains, 'Art is not a luxury but a desperate necessity.'

When it comes to furniture, what advice should one give? You can, of course, choose pieces intended to recount something, to say something. At least to you. But take care to intersperse them with others that are useful, anonymous and silent, so that the whole doesn't generate too deafening a babble. Today a chosen object – be it a lamp, a piece of furniture or any household equipment – can properly do one of two things. It can shout to the four winds what it is trying to tell us; it can be so charged with form, colour and expressive force as to risk being mistaken for an emblem, a piece of sculpture, or even a monument. On the other hand, it can speak under its breath, so softly as to be barely intelligible, but for all that no less convincing. As in one of those English-type friendships, described by Jorge Borges, which begin by excluding intimacy and soon go on to dispense with conversation. And it is the very use of the latter effects, with their extremes of self-effacement and reserve, which permits us to harbour in our houses the former, the emblematic personality-pieces. We cannot have an item of furniture which looks like a monument next to a lamp posing as a piece of sculpture. Their voices would drown each other out. They need the proximity of other objects which possess a secret beauty waiting to be discovered, objects which seem to be made of nothing, or rather, just the essence of an idea.

Avoid the meretriciously modern. In the words of George Santayana, 'those who cannot remember the past are condemned to repeat it'. New forms not fated for instant oblivion almost always evolve from an attentive study of what has gone before.

Only thus will you succeed in having a good house for all seasons. But then, who can say what is really the best? For me, the best house is always the one I have yet to publish.

ISA VERCELLONI

IN THE WAY that much architecture in the 18th century was an expression of civil splendour, and in the 19th a form of celebratory ritual, so today's architecture is a mode of communication. It can communicate ideas, concepts, states of mind, matters of interest both public and private. The architecture featured in Casa Vogue usually conveys a more private message, without excluding general ideas – or at least statements from which general ideas can be inferred. The statements may contradict each other, but that is only because our architectural viewpoint is not fixed. It does not reflect any one tendency but all the restless searchings of our time.

Architect: Mario Botta Photographer: Alo Zanetta

ARCHITECTURE TODAY

EVERYTHING IS CHANGEABLE

Peter D. Eisenman is among the most noted architectural theoreticians to emerge from the American generation that came after Louis Kahn. Besides being founder and director of the Institute for Architecture and Urban Studies, he is an editor of the magazine *Opposition*, and together with M. Graves, J. Heiduck, C. Gwathmey and R. Meier he forms one of the famous 'New York Five'. It was he who, years ago, coined a term for his work which later turned into a slogan: 'Cardboard Architecture'.

Others can decide whether the description fits this recent work in Connecticut. Certainly 'all change' might seem to be its essential message. Rising in the midst of trees, the house does not possess a recognizable façade as such. There is no front and no rear, so it is not possible to spot the main entrance. The walls spring out from every angle. A pillar drops down from above to stop, inexplicably, half a metre from the ground. No respect is shown for any of the conventional building norms. As in nature, there is a feeling of continuous growth and repair, composition and decay. Nothing seems symmetrical. Everything looks purposely incomplete. There is no hierarchical order, no sense of priorities, no set mode of speech. Eisenman has agreed that the whole structure appears to be falling to pieces, and he is said to see buildings as ruins.

Yet – from another view – the structure with its flat roof is of such a mathematical order that it could be turned on its head and still provide virtually the same space. Perhaps this in a way accounts for the staircase that traverses the living room ceiling but leads nowhere – and is coloured red to complement the real staircase, which is green. These two splashes of colour stand out from a quiet background of grey, black and white. One says quiet but only in a manner of speaking, because this is certainly not a house conducive to boredom. Ceiling heights vary within rooms, which also have light coming in from above. Glass walls stretch from top to bottom. From inside, one has a sensation of walking in the open air. At dusk, benign beacons fixed on the roof pour down floods of artificial light. In the house itself there are only candles.

Massimo Vignelli was called on to do the furnishing and carried out his commission in perfect sympathy with the spirit of the place. In the living room, there are four soft mattresses with loose covers that can be put over each other, two and two, so as to become beds. Alternatively they can be spread out over the floor, if the mood of the moment is for a group encounter session; or – should the mood change to relaxed conversation or reading –

The exterior seen from one side. There is no conventional front or back to the house.

they can be rolled up to make the seat and back of a comfortable sofa.

The celebrated Z chairs from a De Stijl design by Gerrit Rietveld – which Cassina has for some seasons now included in the Collezione dei Maestri – show up painted in grey and disposed in a variety of ways: casually aligned to form a bench, encircling a pillar with their backs turned like children put in the corner, or – in a more usual role – set round the dining room table. This last is a versatile piece of furniture which can easily be dismantled if the columns are required for some other use: say, as bases for sculpture or as pedestals for flower arrangements.

Left: a multi-purpose area that can serve as dining room, living room or guest bedroom. Here it is shown as an improvised bedroom with the four dining chairs aligned to form a bench. In the small photographs below: the master bedroom showing the glazed 'cleft' which starts at the ceiling, runs down the wall and in between the two beds along the floor, thus giving light to the living room below.

POST-MODERN CALIFORNIA BEACH STYLE

This house, planned by Fred Fisher – a young architect from Los Angeles – and put up near the beach at Venice, California, is like a collage: a collage of allusions to the local scene, to the personal history of the owner and to the building language of America's West Coast. It is a house charged with symbolism, implications and cultural references, embodied in a bizarre naturalistic form.

Beneath a wooden roof, similar in structure to an old rowing boat, live the Caplins; he a musician, she a sculptor. The former spent fourteen years of his youth in a houseboat on the Seine and this probably accounts for the steep steps with a painted tubular handrail leading up from the ample living area to the bridge, where instead of the captain's cabin we find all the facilities appropriate to a land-based dwelling. Two small porthole windows and a large silvered chimney stack also seem to be survivals of the years spent on the river. And the same goes for all the corners, nooks and niches where a thousand and one objects can be arranged in a confined space.

It is a singular fact that the house lacks a real sitting room, having instead a large central hall like a piazza, an independent meeting place for the two Caplins who both work at home in separate studios.

This is by no means a secretive house, but it shows a decent reticence that many young couples would find congenial. It guarantees privacy in a minimum of space. In the best sense, you could say it was a home-made house.

Left: the principal façade of the Caplins' house arched like a wave caught in motion, with openings dotted here and there in various shapes and sizes and even emerging obliquely from the wall. Left below: the roof-terrace with the strange silvered chimney stack.

In the small pictures below: the double staircase with two ramps of differing slopes, one leading to the bedroom and the other going to the studios; and the kitchen showing the wooden ceiling. Opposite: the doorways connecting the hall with the kitchen/dining room, over which passes a bridge leading to one of the upper floor studios.

A HOUSE AS THEATRE

Anyone approaching the Rodes house, leaving behind the lights of Los Angeles, will find a curved, symmetrical façade full of classical references and strongly reminiscent of a stage set. In front is the proscenium marked with concentric rings in two tones of grey, and there are no less than five French doors for entrances and exits. Before long the show will begin: students and friends of the owner – a professor in love with all things classical and with the theatre – are always welcome to join in. For those who planned the house – Charles Moore together with Ruble and Yudell – the professor was an ideal client who, apart from budgetary considerations, placed no restrictions on their quest for form and made no demands in regard to function. He only wanted something that would be serene, solemn and distinguished – a house that would be a joy to behold. And that is just what he got, even if – according to Charles Jencks, chronicler of post-modern architecture – the Rodes house is only an amusing pastiche that recalls the classicism of the 18th century.

Top left: the stage crescent with two little gazebos on each side. Below: a view of the proscenium, a semicircular platform marked out in alternating shades of grey. Right: the two-storeyed living room with the metal 'passerelle' that runs under the windows and serves to support the lamps and spotlights for illuminating the house's interior and also the outside stage. On the inside wall, a central fireplace and, above, the mezzanine floor. The armchairs are in varying pastel colours and the low oval table is covered with a patchwork quilt. On each side of the fireplace, two passageways leading to the dining room. The ceiling fans add a tropical touch.

A PLEASING ANGLE

With its two wings meeting at right angles, this house has been designed by Marco Zanuso to enclose a patch of meadow that falls away to the edge of nearby Lake Como; and he has given it large expanses of window looking out over the shining water to the fine hilly landscape on the further shore. But approach the house from the back and the welcoming, protective concavity is gone. The roof, which slopes in the other direction, has disappeared as well. The building is sharp and aggressive – like some strategic barrier, like a retaining wall, almost blank except for one or two windows very high up and small as embrasures, just big enough to frame from the inside a view of the upper Como mountain peaks. Or, in other moods, this facet might seem a mere linear structure, without volume, an envelope without thickness, a piece of flat stage scenery, a great screen.

So the house presents an enigmatic and sullen posture to the mountains, but is open and smiling on its other side; and in this it resembles certain gruff specimens of humanity who, when you finally succeed in befriending them, turn out to be the sincerest and most generous of all.

Unusual for Italian architecture is the choice of materials: all wood – except for the primary framework, which is of steel. Pine has been employed for the secondary structure, while shingles of Canadian red cedar (the kind

that goes grey with time) cover the walls and roof.

The L-shaped plan allows a splendidly simple scheme in apportioning the available space: one wing for the parents; the other for the children and – in the attic – the guests. In the parents' wing, on the ground floor, is the living room which can extend out into an open loggia protected by overhanging eaves. Both living room and loggia are paved with Umbrian terracotta tiles. In addition to the attic, there is also a basement which in one wing contains a boathouse and in the other a gymnasium, a workroom and even a corner where the children can put on plays.

Altogether, the house strikes one as an enviably happy place, a result of the creative reaction that now and then occurs when a good architect encounters enlightened clients, the sort of clients who are capable of leading intelligent lives – even while on holiday.

Top left: the side of the house facing the mountains – a compact wall with little windows and a jutting-out staircase. Top right: towards the lake the house opens out like a pair of compasses, gazing out on to a patch of meadow through wide expanses of glass. Below: seen from the back, the house looks like a piece of flat stage scenery – an inch or two thick.

Top left: the living/dining room with kitchen counter in the background. Dining table by Zanuso for Poggi; church seats. Folding shipboard chairs with wooden slats. A swing is suspended by very fine steel wires. Left: the living room seen from behind the kitchen counter. Above: the top of the long kitchen counter which incorporates refrigerator, stoves and cupboards for dishes and cooking utensils – so you can prepare a meal without turning your back on guests. The recess behind the counter houses the sink and dishwasher and can be closed off. On the high ledge, models of the boats which ply Lake Como.

A HOUSE WITH A DOUBLE LIFE

For Napa Valley near San Francisco, Andrew Batey and Mark Mack have designed a neo-primitive type of house encompassing two courtyards and showing two distinct faces to the outside world. To the north, it has the forbidding mien of a small fortress; to the south, it is an open cloister overlooking newly planted vineyards. This enables the occupants to vary their lifestyle from summer to winter, and in fact the building – which incorporates the use of solar panels – has been planned with the regional climate very much in mind.

The architects have utilized advanced building techniques, leaving materials unadorned and free to speak for themselves. The house, with its compact outline, sits well in the local scene.

Inside, the large living/dining room, which looks on to the south courtyard through sliding glass walls, is connected to the north courtyard by a simple central door. Exposed concrete block partitions define the extremities of this living space from the building's two wings (which contain other rooms and the services) but the separation is only a gesture, because the partitions stop short of the sloping ceiling and one side has been left open for ease of communication.

The furniture is all of a piece with the house – almost an extension of it – composed of cement blocks, pedestals, pillars, architraves and so on. This is a current international trend, which views items of furniture as fragments of architecture, as solid set pieces, bringing to our domestic interiors constructional elements hitherto associated primarily with outdoor townscapes.

Left: the building's north front, which faces a wood and consists of two symmetrical, almost blank, castellated blocks separated by a large porch. In contrast, the southern aspect is open and looks through glass walls on to a vineyard. Left below: A view of the north entrance from the interior courtyard. Top right: the area round the living room fireplace with cement benches and a three-legged table with a granite top. Bottom right: a divan with four corners in stepped blocks of cement and terracotta. In the background, the glass walls opening on to the south courtyard and the vineyard.

FORM FOLLOWS FUNCTION

On a suburban residential developm
outside Parma, Guido Canali – an a
who still believes that 'form follows fu
was commissioned to design a few
destined to contrast sharply with th
mash of styles round about. Here a lo
and-white rectangle, hardly visible a
grey surrounding wall, resembles ce
dustrial constructions.

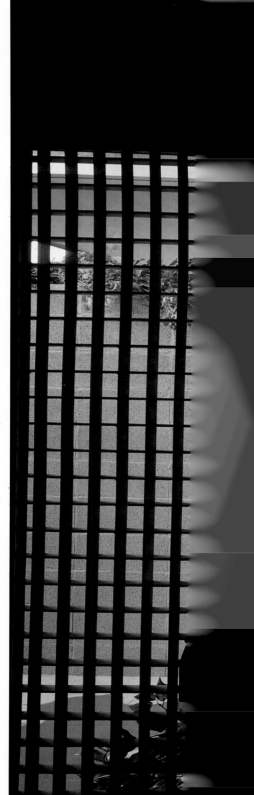

'In the matter of siting', says Canali, 'I wanted to do something as different as possible from all the other houses in the neighbourhood. I wanted to have the building on three sides as close as permissible to the plot boundaries so that the fourth side facing the road could look over the maximum area of secluded garden which would be protected by a high wall. Also, the ground floor has been excavated to set it lower than the natural level. The idea has been to make the house and its occupants look inwards and – except for certain privileged glimpses on the line of its longitudinal axis – to close it off in a sequence of internal patios. The west side is completely blank and the short south side is shielded by a visual filter.'

But Canali's radical choice did not stop there. Through the use of industrial building techniques, he achieved a formal rigour rarely found in Italian houses. The materials are deliberately 'brutal' – pillars and beams in structural galvanized iron, curtain walls in blocks and panels of prefabricated concrete – while inside is a calculated richness of dimension, proportion and views.

Top left: the south side of the house showing the circular iron staircase leading to the solarium and the adjustable panels which serve as a screen against the sun. The living area on the ground floor is sheltered by an arcade. Centre left: the plexiglass-covered pergola leading from the perimeter wall to the front door. Bottom left: the external link running along the first floor sleeping area transformed into two little hanging gardens. Below: a part of the living room seen from the main entrance. Metal trelliswork is used for parking hats, coats and umbrellas.

Left: the dining area extended on to the terrace protected by a draped pergola. Below: the living room seen from the south side. The Flexform sofa in the foreground is composed of six elements, three and three back-to-back. At the end, a fireplace constructed of concrete blocks. At upper floor level, there is a walkway leading to the sleeping area. Above top: the dining area looking towards the kitchen. Seats designed by Enzo Mari and produced by Anonima Castelli. Hanging on the wall, a large canvas in tones of grey, green and white – a work by Ignazio Moncada.

The kitchen divided into a working area and a glassed-in cabin for the actual cooking.

A sort of hatchway leading to one of the bathrooms. The lighting comes from above, through a plexiglass dome on the roof.

THE HOUSE WITH A GLASS HEART

The rapport between a building and its setting has always been an important element in the work of Mario Botta, an architect from Ticino in Switzerland who has been practising since the 1970s, specializing in the design of private houses. In the example shown here, the steeply sloping terrain constitutes a significant starting point for a building whose most striking characteristics are its unusual façade and its transparent core surmounted by a vaulted skylight. Set against a hillside at Viganello, in Ticino, the house seems to be hooked on to the sloping ground, with its curved back wall producing in the living room a sort of exedra, which is also open at the ceiling. A massive central brickwork pillar runs vertically through the whole construction, forming an apex to the upper-floor triangular patio which overlooks the valley. Another triangle, with chopped-off corners, presiding over a brief flight of steps, makes an impressive opening to the entrance hall.

Of particular decorative interest is the architect's idea of patterning the façade with bricks inserted at an angle of 45°. This breaks the surface with a sort of visual vibration and produces an effect of chiaroscuro which changes according to the position of the sun.

Both outside and inside, it is the play of light that lends most enchantment to this house with a glass heart.

Top left: this foreshortened view of the façade shows the chiaroscuro effect obtained with bricks inserted at an angle of 45°. Bottom left: the trapezial shaped entrance and above it the patio which is covered by the domed skylight. Below: the living room with 'Squash' sofa by Deganello for Driade and chair by Botta for Alias. Right: the house centres round a great brickwork pillar which runs the entire height and dominates the patio, which can be closed off from the weather by sliding glass doors.

A KIND OF GATEHOUSE

In this example of rural architecture, designed by Afra and Tobia Scarpa, a transparent house on the one hand and a courtyard for living in on the other seem to be discreetly swapping roles.

The whole complex – laid out to meet local zoning regulations, which severely limit housing densities but allow more latitude for buildings devoted to other uses – is divided into three sections: the house in front, a long structure like a traditional open-sided barn at the rear, and in between an open space that could be called a courtyard but has been planned really as an extension to the two buildings and treated with the same architectural care.

In the house, four central rooms – situated on two floors with windows running the whole height and framed by great expanses of masonry – appear like four gateways, through which the surrounding countryside joins up with the courtyard behind. There – in the courtyard – blocks of porphyry are used to pave the part set aside for vehicles: the centre is occupied by a great expanse of grass with two large, square, shallow pools dotted with water-lilies where swallows splash about.

The solid walls of the house have been faced with prefabricated panels of pinkish cement, vertically ridged to produce a decorative pattern from the play of light and shade. The cement panels covering the walls of the 'barn' which look away from the courtyard are grey and have been scored horizontally. The difference in colour has been chosen deliberately to give the enclosed area a warmer tone.

Despite its modern style, the project really harks back to old peasant forms, with the dwelling as a gatehouse leading to an enclosed courtyard beyond. This particular courtyard has the silent magic and the poetic dimension of a cloister. Whatever may happen outside, here you are sheltered. However much the surrounding area may one day be built up, here there is a meadow.

The project has many virtues, including a precise and balanced ordering of space and mass, a general harmony of proportion, and careful attention to detail throughout. However, none of these in itself would have generated any unique quality had the architects not also contributed a deep and loving insight into the countryside – with its rhythms, its charms and its problems.

Above: the side of the house overlooking the courtyard. The transparent parts have been planned to act as a kind of filter between courtyard and countryside. The opaque surfaces are faced with panels of pinkish cement. The roofs are finished in copper. In front of the house can be seen the two large pools. Above right: the garage 'barn' at the opposite end of the courtyard with another view of the two pools showing the water-lilies. Right: the dining room enclosed by two walls of glass and two of exposed brick. Wooden-beamed ceilings and a floor of trachyte. Table and seats by Afra and Tobia Scarpa for Maxalto and B&B Italia. Flos lamps.

33

Above, and bottom right: a grey lacquer built-in storage unit running the whole height separates the parents' sleeping area from their private sitting room. On the bedside tables, *two Biagio marble lamps by Tobia Scarpa produced by Flos. The false ceiling in the sitting room and the cupboards in the bedroom are of light-coloured birchwood. The* *leather armchairs are Coronado from B&B Italia and the chaise-longue is a Le Corbusier model reissued by Cassina. Above right: the passage from the dining area to the living*

. The ceiling shows the outline of beams
d in by panels of birchwood. On the
g room wall a tapestry executed to a
n by Mark Tobey.

PARALLELISM

What strikes one first about the house designed by Gianni Braghieri and built at Appiano Gentile, near Como, is its spare simplicity. In essence it has been laid out in the form of an 'H', with two long rectangles linked by a corridor-cum-conservatory. The rectangle to the left comprises the day area, with a kitchen/dining room divided from the living room by back-to-back fireplaces and a stairway coming up from the cellar garage. The right-hand wing has three bedrooms and two bathrooms strung out along a straight passageway.

The austerity of the ground plan is carried through the whole design. Roof-trusses flaunt their geometry, floors come in large terracotta slabs, plain white plaster finishes the walls. And there are the square windows which separate into four neat panes.

One would be hard put to imagine a more practical house than this one, but – as so often

happens – something that works well has sprung more from architectural flair than from a preoccupation with functionalism *per se*.

The entire concept has the compass and completeness of what, in music, would be dubbed a 'short piece'. It also has an engaging naivete, a bit as if a child were depicting a house in categorical, symbolic terms, rather than a literal representation.

Above: the house's two symmetrical wings, comprising day and night areas, connected by a glassed-in passageway. Below: in the winter, the link is used also as a greenhouse. Above right: the living room with two sofas placed back-to-back, one looking towards the windows, the other towards the fireplace. Below right: the kitchen showing the centre table covered in traditional geometrically patterned tiles.

TOP OF THE HILL

Built in 1970 by Gianugo Polesello on the site of an old lookout post belonging to the fief of the Castello d'Arcano, this is a house situated at the furthest limit of the morainic hill-slopes which describe an amphitheatre surveying the valleys and the plain of Friuli's River Tagliamento.

The building – clear and uncompromising in style – is an intensely personal statement from Polesello, who has drawn deeply on the experience of his own father's house and another house where he lived later in the low-lying Friuli countryside. What is more, it was designed for a medical practitioner with whom Polesello had been close friends at high school

and seems in a way to be the practical culmination of what were once shared boyhood dreams.

The structure is of steel and reinforced concrete, and the basic concept is that of a double shell. There is easy access to the flat roof, where even a telescope is available for those wishing to gaze across to the Adriatic. The floors contained by the inner shell are like two blocks of differing shape placed one on top of the other with only one lateral aspect forming a simple rectangle – that is the elevation with the brise-soleil which faces towards the west. The exposed east-facing side – only one storey high owing to the lie of the land – is taken up by the living room, long and shallow as a verandah, outside which has been erected a well-designed pergola, a bit similar to Mies van der Rohe's garden architecture but also reminiscent of those traditional Italian traps devised to net migrating birds.

The hall, like a small carriage-way, was intended to provide for the young on their motorbikes, but now has a wax-polished floor.

The house's interior plan is broadly along three parallel lines, in the manner of a typical Palladian villa – only that here there is a circulatory surround which puts the day and night areas into closer contact with each other.

Top left: the south front approached by the driveway that ascends to the top of the hill. The west-facing brise-soleil can be glimpsed on the left. Bottom left: the east side seen through the pergola. Right: a view of the stairway from the upper landing looking towards the bridge which leads directly from the living room to one of the bedrooms. The window at the back is of thick glass protected by the large squares of a metal grill. Below: the living room on the upper floor, which runs the whole length of the east side. It has three connections with the sleeping area, one of which can be seen on the right.

THEATRICAL ILLUSIONS

'Everything is built on sand, nothing is built on stone, but we must build on sand as though it were stone.' This quotation from Borges, used by Gae Aulenti to introduce her work in the exhibition 'Italy: the New Domestic Landscape' held at the Museum of Modern Art, New York in 1972, seems to apply particularly to the house shown here. Situated on the outskirts of a small Tuscan city, it is framed by eight parallel walls staggered rather in the manner of stage wings and pierced at different points in an ingenious number of ways. Aulenti's past collaboration with Luca Ronconi and her involvement – *inter alia* – with the Theatre Workshop of Prato have obviously left their mark. There is nothing in the least ephemeral or improvised about this piece of architecture but the theatrical element is very evident. For instance, it is difficult to recall sometimes quite whether you are indoors or out. The walls are all the same, all in brick; and the rooms, courtyards and corridors resemble equally a closed domestic interior or the exterior spaces of an intimate townscape. There is, moreover, a touch of theatrical illusion in the way the house isolates itself from what is going on in the suburban quarter where it stands. By contrast, it has an intimate rapport with both earth and sky, especially the latter with which it communes through great streaks of glass let into the roof. The walls don't overdo their

pretence of being stage wings. For practical everyday purposes they define rooms imaginatively, but quite firmly. The building's natural and enduring materials – wood, brick, terracotta, stone – also have an authoritative tone and will, in time, give shape to the days and the years, expressing in simple, silent terms the relationship which existed between those who conceived and built the house and those who live in it.

Above and below right: two views of the only room that has been planned on a really grand scale. The effect is of a cascade with the different areas – eating, conversation, study – following one after the other. The dividing line between indoors and outdoors is blurred in a number of ways – by the streaks of daylight from the ceiling, the narrow openings on the left looking on to the little patio and the negative bay-window further back. In the background below, 'Zig Zag' tables and seats designed by Rietveld and produced by Cassina. Sofa and chairs with blue-painted steel frames and cavalry twill upholstery – also revolving chair – by Le Corbusier (Cassina). Above left: a detail of the large room with the fireplace which is open on every side. Seen through the fireplace, a small painter's studio.

IN A WORLD as built-up as ours is, we are usually destined to live within walls that already have a past. This past may be recent and anonymous (as in a rented flat put up during Italy's construction boom of the 1950s) or remote and well documented (as in an 18th-century villa in Lombardy or the summer pavilion of a German Schloss). But whether anonymous or laden with other people's memories, our houses can always be rendered more alive and relevant to ourselves, provided there is a thread of mutual affinity running through the decoration and contents, however disparate – in period, provenance and style – the individual items may be.

Architect: Francesco Soro Photographer: Carla De Benedetti

TODAY IN AN OLD HOUSE

A TRANSFORMABLE APARTMENT

The layout of this long, narrow, rectangular loft at the top of a hundred-year-old building in the heart of Greenwich Village was the brain-child of the well-known furniture textile designer, Jack Lenor Larsen, who lives there. The detailed work of conversion was done by Don Davidson of Charles Forberg Associates, with furnishing by Sam Takeuchi of Takony Form and Design, using Japanese workmen.

The result is a little museum of craftsmanship with an unmistakable Japanese touch, and with multi-purpose areas that can be transformed at will. Structural alterations have been kept to a minimum. Walls have been whitewashed, and the brick vaults of the ceiling have been left exposed to view. At the ends of the apartment, however, there have been constructed platforms raised to window height and looking like two little stages. On these the play can change from moment to moment according to the items of furniture used: oriental easy chairs, a low dining table, or perhaps a comfortable sleeping mattress. Things not currently needed can be stored under the platforms.

Right: one of the many versions of this protean apartment. The dais at the end, with storage space underneath, has a fireplace on the right hand side and can be used for sitting – Japanese-style – on low wicker seats or (as illustrated overleaf) for sleeping. On the left side of the dais there is a pool. Below: the pool overlooks the roof-terrace and by day reflects the sky. The walls of the main room are lined with shelves that can be concealed by sliding doors. Cocktail trolley by Alvar Aalto for Artek.

Overleaf: in the second room there is another dais below the window, on it a Japanese hand-loom for weaving textile prototypes. In the corner, a pottery bowl by Jim Owen. Fabrics, rugs and matting by Jack Larsen. Right: a mattress placed on the dais of the first room; on the shelves pieces of modern glass by Dale Chihuly; lighted candles floating on the surface of the pool.

A VARIETY
OF REFERENCES

How odd to find this apartment, with its emotive and multi-coloured decor, lurking in an anonymous block of flats in a small town near Salerno! Redone by Nunzio Vitale and Saverio Caiazza, it has art deco and 1940s pieces happily coexisting with more recent trail blazers and an allusion or two to minimal art. In addition to the unlikely setting, other contrasts stand out: for instance, a section of coloured ceramic floor tiles, of traditional local make, inserted like a square rug into a banal expanse of herring-bone parquet: or the

wall tiles in the bathroom which crumble away and evoke the peeling façades of the SITE group. But these jarring notes are intended to stimulate. The references are deliberately overlapped and mixed. 'Things get jumbled up in the memory,' says Vitale. 'This is all part of the creative tension of design and helps to sustain its impulse.'

Below: the living room, sparsely furnished with a few important pieces. In the foreground, an easy chair complete with footrest by Poltrona Frau. Elsewhere, a rare lacquered wood Schmied screen of 1925, an art deco table with 1940s vases, and – on the wall – a work by Tony Cress entitled The Bird. *Standard lamp by Ingo Maurer. Bottom right: the living room has been enlarged by incorporating the old entrance hall. Stools by Alvar Aalto (Artek) and bar by Gio Ponti,*

1940. On the wall, a work by Francesco Matarrese. Top right: 'stage curtains' mounted on a semicircular runner.

Overleaf left: the floor of multi-coloured ceramic tiles made in Vietri continues from living room to kitchen. Note the triangular console table in marble, metal, ceramic and wood, designed by Nunzio Vitale and Ugo Marano; also the Danish roll-top storage unit from Pastoe and the round iron tables by Castiglioni from Zanotta. Right: close-ups of the two Castiglioni tables. Top right: a bathroom showing the wall tiles deliberately peeling away and a mirror with hand-painted glass. Bottom right: another bathroom with a tub decorated in mosaic by Ugo Marano. Through the window can be seen a landscape 'decorated' by the illustrious 18th-century architect Luigi Vanvitelli.

A HALFWAY HOUSE

A young couple moved into one of the many small villas with gardens that were laid out round Milan during the first half of this century and called on Ettore Sottsass to put it in order for them. 'Should we make structural alterations?' they asked. 'Should we pull down walls and add new rooms?' 'Don't do anything,' the architect replied. 'In a few years you'll have amassed so many books and had so many babies, you won't be able to stay on here anyway.' So instead he designed for them fantastic refrigerators tricked out in pink-and-white dots, jardinières like miniature temples, pink-and-blue neon snakes, columns and canopies in mock marble, fragile monuments in glass and fake granite ... One of these monuments, a kind of magical luminous mast, a welcoming, fervidly-coloured totem pole, stands right in the middle of the entrance hall and immediately lends the house its distinctive

tone. Imposing to view, it's delicate in substance – and will be easy to carry away, when books and babies have become too thick on the ground and it's time to move on again. Meanwhile, the house has been refurbished with deft and imaginative touches, and the owners have been spared all the expense of major changes to the fabric. A light-hearted and stylish philosophy of make-do has cut their problems down to size.

Left and centre: an archway decorated with neon lighting and a kind of magical totem pole are the first things that greet visitors to the house. Below top: blue-painted beams in the attic music room; and bottom: a great canopy of shamelessly mock marble in the bedroom.

MUTUAL AFFINITIES

The apartment is situated a few miles from Milan, in one wing of an 18th-century villa said to have been at least partly the work of Giuseppe Piermarini. The owner moved here just over ten years ago, allowing the children to grow up freely in a countrified atmosphere. The family called on the advice of an architect friend, Antonio Piva, who suggested keeping everything much as it was. The place was by no means neglected: some of the interior bore spur of the moment – ended up contributing happily to the total effect. From time to time, other things were added: the odd antique piece or modern furniture designed by Tobia and Afra Scarpa, who also created the striking iron and brass chimney in the dining room.

As viewed now, the whole blends perfectly because governed by a balanced and discriminating taste. As in friendships, there is an accord founded on respect and affinity.

signs of having been done up in the late 19th century, and another architect (Caccia Dominioni) had put in work on it at the end of World War II. So the irregular ceiling heights were retained, and no drastic alterations were made to the late Victorian (or Umbertine) decorations on the staircase. Walls were tinted in a fitting shade of periwinkle blue.

In the event, everything worked out well. The house and the new contents took to each other in a spirit of common sympathy. Everything brought in – including furniture from the family's previous home in Milan plus pieces of majolica, glass and old prints bought on the

Above: the front of the villa overlooking the local piazza. The original fabric goes back to 1777, but the building was given a face-lift in the late 19th century, and recently the roof has been redone using old tiles. Right: the staircase with marbled surfaces and decorations in an eclectic style typical of the 19th century. Opposite: the long entrance gallery, paved in black and white squares, becomes a hothouse in winter for potted citrus plants. Sirrah light fittings from the Albini-Helg-Piva studio. Through the opening at the end can be glimpsed an art nouveau settee and a female portrait c.1920.

Above and right: the living room with its artificially grained ceiling – a feature retained in the recent redecoration. Two tall passageways, one on each side of the marble fireplace, have been opened up and lead to the gallery. Antique pieces mix perfectly with contemporary furniture such as Maxalto sofas and B&B Italia armchairs. On the wall a tapestry by Campendonk, on the floor an 'art carpet' by Mauro Reggiani. Left: the dining room with the iron and brass chimney designed by Tobia Scarpa and silverware by San Lorenzo.

A BLENDING
OF OLD AND NEW

Architects Lorenzo Prando and Riccardo Rosso – both Piedmontese and in their forties, working as interior designers – play a subtle game of irony and snobbism. Their inspiration stems from 19th-century interior scenes painted in watercolour by such artists as Garnerey, Pelez and Macdonald, or from court snapshots taken at a time when reigning families were beginning to become bourgeois in their everyday habits: 'in those daily gestures that constitute the fabric of life', as Prando and Rosso put it. And it is in this mood, open to references and memories from the past, that they have restored and furnished a small mansion in the hills just outside Turin.

The longer and narrower side of the house, which ends in a neo-Gothic turret decorated in bands of grey and red (shades deduced from other exteriors in the neighbourhood and from traces of colour that still remained), was once a convent and dates back to the 17th century. The rest of the structure was added in the first years of the 19th century. So the building, in a sense, was ready-made for these architects, who – interpreting the tastes of their clients (he a collector of contemporary art, she an enthusiastic grower of succulent plants, both of them country lovers) – have transformed it into a comfortable home where old and new blend in a spirit of the most pleasing eclecticism. Period pieces, revitalized by colour, mix in

perfect harmony with modern objects and custom-designed items of furniture. Additional colour – and a touch of *gravitas* – is supplied by modern works of art chosen *ad hoc*. Certain furniture pieces in common use do not hide their purpose but positively assert it with simple lines and the choice of honest materials (sheet metal, laminates, light-coloured woods, etc.). Ease of arrangement has been given high priority, as with the sofas on casters, the multi-tiered jardinières – also on casters – and the free-standing bookcases in the living room. All this allows the rooms to be crowded without sacrificing adaptability and convenience – a *sine qua non* for the exigencies of everyday life.

Above: the house seen from the meadow. The white part ending in the neo-Gothic turret – which is painted in grey and red stripes according to local custom – was originally a 17th-century convent. The part painted red is an early 19th-century addition. Right: the living room fashioned out of three small communicating rooms knocked into one. The far table is Louis Philippe and the nearer one is a specially designed modern piece. On the back wall, a Pistoletto mirror-picture and a neo-classical earthenware stove. Photographer's lamps and multi-tiered jardinières on casters.

Left: the kitchen with various old Thonet chairs placed round a large table. The table itself and the two pieces set against the walls (of beechwood and marble on the left, simple *beechwood on the right) were designed by the architects. Top: the master bedroom with two 18th-century wardrobes painted in different colours and with the initials of the two* *owners. The iron bedstead is Genoese. Art déco rugs on the floor. Small pictures from left to right: a bathroom, one of the children's bedrooms, and a small private sitting room.*

who gazes down from the wall. The butler'
pantry is full of nothing but pottery. In th
library – where there are more white vase
than books – a 'flying carpet' armchair ha
landed in front of two little seats and a table b
Rietveld. Then there is the study – but coul
anyone work seriously at a table claiming to b
a 'crazy horse'? In the bedroom, Bauhau
influences have damped down the natura
exuberance of Ceroli (and we can only hope th
'mouth of truth' stays mum). There is also
large living/dining room (a suite of thre
rooms) crowded with disturbing juxtaposition
of gelatinous furniture pieces and sever
chrome-plated steel frames. What on eart
became of the dwarf, one wonders, who used t
sit in the minute Thonet chair watching th
Zanuso television plonked down on th
Charles Eames table?

A CAREFREE
COLLECTION

Sorgenfrei (meaning 'sans-souci' or 'carefree')
is a pavilion in the grounds of Hünnefeld
castle, near Bad Essen, in Westphalia. The
castle itself – seat of the aristocratic von dem
Bussche-Hünnefeld family – goes back to the
12th century, although the main body dates
from 1740 and was restored and partially
reconstructed in 1825. It was then that an
architect of the neo-classical school built a
pavilion, which was first intended as a summer
residence but later became a dower house for
widows *and* widowers (in accordance with a
North German custom observed also among
the peasantry). The pavilion continued as a
dower house until 1921, when it was left
untenanted and fell into dilapidation. Then in
the spring of 1976 Rainer Krause, together
with a friend, decided to rent and restore it,
furnishing it with his modern design collection: German pieces of the 1930s, Americana of
the 1950s (his first love) and Italian pieces of
the 1960s and 1970s. Just lately, he has added
some things of more recent date (seats and
armchairs, pottery lamps and other acces-
sories) besides interesting pieces of a 'poetic
function' (Sottsass pottery, miniature models,
old fragments and miscellaneous finds).

Now, at Sorgenfrei, furniture and objects
have been disposed almost as though in a
gallery. In the entrance hall with its floor of
Fettstein (a kind of stone treated with pig's fat),
there is a tiny chest of drawers by von Klier
topped by a mini-cactus, and – next to a tribute
to Andy Warhol – a Sottsass 'superbox' to hide
the overcoats from the sight of Le Corbusier

Opposite above: the front of the pavilion in the grounds of Hünnefeld castle. Opposite below: the entrance hall with a little chest of drawers by von Klier for Planula of 1969, and at the end of the corridor a striped wardrobe by Ettore Sottsass for Poltronova (1968). Left: one of the living rooms with other furniture pieces by Sottsass and by Charles Eames (of 1947 and 1953) with a Thonet doll's chair in front of a television set by Zanuso for Brionvega. Below: the end of the study adjoining the bedroom with a chair by Eames and a set of shelves and pottery by Sottsass. The bed with the carved head is by Mario Ceroli for Poltronova. The house has many other rooms where German pieces of the 1930s, Americana of the 1950s and Italian designs running from 1960 to 1980 have shaken down together with their common bond of quality and creativity.

AS MENTIONED in the previous section, our private address is more often than not a place with a past. Usually this place with a past was conceived from the word go as a home; but at times – especially in cities where residential districts are changing their shape and character – you may find yourself choosing to live in what was once a warehouse or a factory or a workshop, or even a church. These places, with their proportions which seem at first glance so unsuited to domestic life, offer a particularly exciting challenge to the imagination and ingenuity of those who have the task of adapting them to their new use.

Architect: Toni Cordero Photographer: Carla De Benedetti

CHANGES OF USE

and Cerutti have also achieved something many might have thought impossible. Far from detracting from the interior's monumentality, they have respected and enhanced it while at the same time reconciling it with the requirements of everyday living – and in an uncanny fashion they have given it a thoroughly human scale.

Left: the façade with the glass and iron gallery added at ground level. Below: a view of the apse taken from upper floor level, showing platforms erected at differing heights (the one running the length of the building being deliberately off-centre) and with spiral

staircase in the foreground. The two large urns are late 18th century and once stood at the foot of a grand ceremonial stairway. The brass bowl is 19th century, from Thailand. Opposite: a view looking towards the entrance. In the foreground, a 16th-century Venetian statue of painted wood (one of a couple, the other standing opposite but outside the photograph). In the background on the left, a marble table by Carlo Scarpa for Simon International and picture by Fabrizio Clerici. Art nouveau candlestick and 18th-century Murano glass chandelier. On the upper floor, a Charles X bookcase. At the bottom of the spiral staircase, a large picture by Francis Bacon.

A CONVERTED CHURCH

Architects Toni Cordero and Jannot Cerutti have taken what was once an obscure London church and turned it into a private dwelling of considerable distinction and style. Erected in 1845, the church was later deconsecrated and underwent various vicissitudes, including being used as an artist's atelier and a television studio. Understandably, no excessive respect was shown for the building's fabric, and the most obvious result of this may be seen in the insensitive alterations to the façade with the two intrusive openings running up to cornice level. Authentic restoration would have been difficult because, apart from anything else, no solid evidence could be found showing how the exterior had looked before. The architects' solution, therefore, was to leave the façade more or less as it was but, in a sense, to distance themselves from it by adding on the ground floor a narrow gallery of glass and iron incorporating a new, modestly sized front entrance. As for the interior, this presented another kind of problem: the church had been conceived with a somewhat unusual plan, having an apse and a space that seemed proportioned for a nave and two side aisles but was in fact undivided: dignified perhaps, but hardly an ideal domestic setting. The architects dealt with this in an original and effective manner. The spatial unity was maintained, but the insertion of strategically placed cement half-walls and beautifully designed overhead walkways means that you virtually never obtain a global view. In exchange, you are offered a series of charming perspectives and something that constitutes an exciting piece of interior architecture in its own right. Cordero

*Another view of the upper-floor gallery
showing the arrangement of windows.*

MORE AFFECTION THAN RESPECT

It used to be the service courtyard of an old palazzo in the Brera district of Milan, one of those enclosures to which the carriages would retire to stand under the portico, having stopped just long enough in the main courtyard to allow the gentry to alight. Now it has been turned into a secret winter garden serving as a studio apartment for two young people in the business of producing television films – an innovative type of job that doesn't fit in with established behaviour patterns, where work and leisure tend to mix and where private and social lives also merge.

The structural conversion and interior design were undertaken by architect Vittorio Garatti, who – undoubtedly owing to many years spent in Latin America, first in Venezuela and then in Cuba, where he worked from 1961 to 1973 – has a fondness for the tropical dwelling where all rooms open on to a central patio. And that is how he planned the apartment, with a large central space which is simultaneously a patio, a private courtyard and a piazzetta, where the natural light streams in from above (so that the plants grow almost as if in an outside garden) and where one can talk, have parties, listen to music, read, even study. There is also a sleeping area in full view, which can just as conveniently be put to daytime use. Along three sides runs the portico/corridor/hall which leads to other rooms: guest rooms or small studios where anyone can go when they need more privacy, or if they have some specific work to do – as in the cutting room or in the music and monitoring room, which doubles as a meeting room and dining room.

Garatti has taken full account of the occupants' specialized lifestyle without ignoring the place's past. He has not, however, allowed himself to be too conditioned by what went before. Coffered ceilings, cornices, plaster work, etc., have all been restored where appropriate; but the fragile domed skylight – in glass and iron, like a greenhouse – has been replaced by an accessible flat roof of concrete-framed glass blocks. Freshly constructed arches, columns, pilasters and mouldings have been

Above left: a view of the outside garden. Left: one of the windows furnished with a school type blind. Right: the former courtyard covered in with a ceiling of concrete-framed glass blocks. The column in granite is the only one to have survived from the old portico. The room-dividing shelves constructed of narrow wooden slats have been painted white to add to the garden atmosphere. 'Dinamo' sofas are by Zanotta; chairs are by Verner Panton for Fritz Hansen; the jardinière on the left, in steel and plastic laminate, is a reissue by Zanotta of a 1930s piece by Levi-Montalcini and Pagano.

put where similar structures probably once existed; yet the new white columns make no attempt to match the one authentic surviving example, which towers proudly over everyone in its grey-gold uniform of old granite. And then – to give a greater sense of space and continuity with the outside – a false French door, created out of looking-glass, has been put at a blank end of the porticoed corridor.

So the past has been extended more affection than respect: it has been treated familiarly as something to be freely – some might say even intemperately – exploited in order to establish a satisfactory dialogue with the present.

Above: one of the small studios planned to provide privacy. Seats by Castiglioni for Zanotta, armchair by Eames. Right: the dining room which is also used for meetings, listening to the hi-fi and monitoring videotapes. To improve the acoustics, sound-absorbent panels have been placed along the walls. Seats are by Arne Jacobsen for Fritz Hansen. Reflecting the owners' occupation, film-reel container lids have been used for table mats.

Below: the entrance hall with a picture by Lucio Del Pezzo over a wicker-work settee.
Right: a view of the portico/corridor near the entrance hall, with two benches by Pistoletto for Megalopoli and on the wall a 'multiple' by Luciano Fabro.

Right: another part of the corridor where doors lead off to the studios (or guest rooms). At the end a false French door creates an illusion of added length. A sleeping area can be seen round the corner. Far right: the sleeping area in greater detail. Bed by Magistretti for Flou, 'Arco' lamp by Castiglioni for Flos, corner cupboard by Matteo Thun for Memphis, pictures by Mimmo Rotella and Pasotti. Above the bed is a rolled up screen for film projection.

HIGH TECH IN
THE QUARTIER BASTILLE

Some years after his Pop inspired 'mo-pad', and following a Magritte phase (tufts of cloud and doves scattered all over furniture and walls), the photographer Uwe Ommer, sensitive as always to swings of taste, was one of the first in Paris to import the High Tech style already current in the SoHo lofts of New York City. Here, in a former furniture warehouse in the Quartier Bastille where Ommer lives, the hard look of supertechnology has been conveyed with a coating of black on walls and ceiling, with stamped rubber, steel, wire netting and burlap for the fittings, and with storehouse lamps and a large billiard table such as you might find in a public pool-room. The only real lapse from hard High Tech style is the earth-coloured overall carpet, a concession to the irresistible claims of homely comfort.

Left: three storehouse lamps shine down on the billiard table in the living area. The few items of furniture have all been made to the owner's design out of materials with industrial connotations – for example, square steel tubing and wire netting for the sofa, with cushions upholstered in burlap packing cloth as used by New York household removal firms. The low table, with its top of bullet-proof glass set on rubber wheels, has perhaps been taken from a more sophisticated version by Gae Aulenti. Walls and ceiling are painted black. Japanese type window-blinds. Below opposite: other details of the living area with a view of the sofa from behind. Immediately below: a corner of the bar upholstered in black stamped rubber and equipped with ordinary bar stools. Stamped rubber has also been used for the floor of the bedroom, which is equipped with a sunken bath.

BETWEEN
TOWN AND ARCADIA

With the blinds up – or should one say with the theatre curtain raised? – this studio apartment belonging to Flavio Albanese (man of taste, interior decorator, designer and scenographer) is for all the world a lighted stage. The scene shifts from living-room to studio to bedroom, where – in the best theatrical tradition – the play's final act unfolds. All this has been created out of an old greenhouse, a former orangery, standing in the grounds of the Palazzo Angaran-Vaccari in Vicenza, whose façade was planned for Bernardo da Schio in 1565 by Andrea Palladio.

The windows, while giving a showcase effect from the outside, also bring the interior into intimate contact with the garden – which extends, through rose beds surrounded by unclipped trees, down to the River Bacchiglione.

On the terrace, a long swathe of white cloth is loosely draped over pairs of metal columns painted in various shades ranging from lilac to deep violet. The same end of the spectrum has been raided for the interior, with azure floors and walls limewashed in a particular tint of pale blue.

Far left: the gateway, dated 1565 and attributed to Palladio, which separates the main courtyard of the Angaran-Vaccari from the garden. Statues are the work of Orazio Marinali. Left: a view of the roof-terrace with painted metal columns supporting the canopy of white cloth. Reclining chairs by Pedano. Below: the apartment as it appears at night from the garden. From left to right, the bedroom, bathroom and the big studio-cum-living room.

In the small photographs: the area used as a studio with hi-fi equipment and, below, the kitchen which was once the stable. (Note the old trough, now used as a shelf, made of local stone.) Nineteenth-century Veneto cupboard.
In the large photograph: an Oikos room divider from Driade placed between the dining area and the entrance hall and displaying a choice collection of Murano glass.

SERENITY IN SPACE

Architects Gastone Del Greco and Luciano Grassi, presented with an agglomeration of buildings grown up over the years round a focal point of what was probably a 13th-century watch tower, have sensitively converted this rambling rural complex into a comfortable and conspicuously functional home. Of the tower itself – in the countryside near Florence – there remains only the base, and one imagines that the superstructure collapsed in an earthquake which shook the district towards the end of the last century. However, the surviving buildings possess features of

Top: a view from the back where the architects have reopened old walled-up windows, putting in iron bars and balconies of metal grating to distinguish the new work. Above: a more general view of the sprawling farm buildings constructed round a medieval nucleus. Right: the internal courtyard, paved in terracotta. The Driade tables have cement bases. Far right: the basement with a Bric room-divider from Driade to demarcate the studio and sleeping areas. Table also from Driade. In the niche at the back, a Sirrah lamp taken from an old design by Man Ray.

Overleaf: the living room with a large
fireplace of modern proportions. Pollena sofas
by Enzo Mari for Driade. Beside the fireplace,
two cache-pots reissued by Bieffeplast from a
pattern by Hoffmann.

much character and charm which the restorers
have fully respected – especially the thick
main walls with their irregular surfaces.
Where dangerous floors have had to be re-
paired, the work has been carried out with
salvaged materials. Unexpected niches and
blocked-up openings, both external and internal, which came to light only with the removal
of old plaster work, have been put back as they
once were. Where new partitions and other
essential structures have been added, the
alterations have been made honestly and without equivocation, utilizing – for example –

unclad iron girders and panels of industrial
metal grating.

For furnishing, a single sectional system –
Bric by Driade – has been chosen for its
adaptability to different shapes and functions:
also, individual contemporary pieces of great
simplicity.

The general effect is of a serenity far
removed from the noise and bustle of urban
life. This is not to imply that the owners have
only a contemplative love of the country: they
made the move here primarily to run a modern
agricultural business.

Left: a room with a mezzanine floor and a spiral staircase. The column of sectional components is from Driade, as is the glass and metal table designed by Enzo Mari. The 'Monofilo' seats have been designed by the two architects who carried out the restoration. On

this page: the kitchen containing a great cylindrical oven which opens on to the courtyard. Furniture is from Driade (Gabbialibera wall units, a Capitello table and Delfina seats). Studio bedrooms are furnished from Driade as well, except for the 'Monofilo' chairs. One of the rooms has a mezzanine floor with a framework made of industrial grating.

LOWER EAST SIDE LOFT

The loft where Antonio Morello and Donato Savoie live occupies two floors of an 1870s Greek Revival building in New York's Lower East Side between SoHo, Lafayette Street and Little Italy. Wanting a complete contrast from their working environment, which is strewn with papers and books and the many appurtenances of their profession, Morello and Savoie –

architects of the Studio Morsa partnership – have deliberately set about creating an effect of emptiness and visual tranquillity. The apartment's sleeping area, situated on a mezzanine floor of the utmost simplicity, is reached by a white painted corkscrew staircase. Beneath the mezzanine is a large kitchen/dining area, equipped to the standards of a commercial restaurant, where the two owners can savour one of life's profounder pleasures: sharing a taste for good cooking with friends.

Top: the double row of windows seen from the freshly constructed mezzanine floor. Above left: the kitchen/dining area situated under the mezzanine. Table and benches are 18th-century Sicilian. Above right: a wooden statue of the same period at the end of the passageway leading to the sauna. Right: another view of the windows curtained by a giant square of parachute silk. In the foreground, the spiral staircase leading to the sleeping area on the mezzanine floor.

'CONCEPTUAL' CONVERSION

In that part of the Maremma which runs almost flat between orchards and olive groves along the Via Aurelia near the coast at Follonica, there is an ancient farmhouse inhabited by the architect Giancarlo Bicocchi. Originally, Bicocchi had intended it as just a holiday home, but the ambience proved to be so congenial that he and his family now live there most of the time.

Restoration was carried out gradually as and when the need seemed to arise, and great respect has been paid to the existing structure.

Even the square French windows have been provided with fanlights where these existed before in the old cowshed; because what is now the living room, kitchen and studio was once used for keeping cattle and storing farm implements. The cement floor – which was sloped – has now been levelled, waterproofed, and finished in white road-paint together with all the other floors of the house. The walls, in tribute to a shade that was already there in one of the little rooms, have been colour-washed in a limpid, clear sky-blue. Furniture is very basic. Almost everything can be moved, dismantled, packed up, unpacked and reassembled if need be; far from being a binding, formal element, it is treated as a simple fact of everyday life. The house – full of colour, children and animals – has an abundantly lived-in atmosphere; and friends, who are always welcome, are also free to make their own contributions to the decor. The most evident of these are two Conceptual works by Daniel Buren on the walls at each end of the living room.

Below left: the living room seen from the loggia. Below right: the doorway, leading from the living room (once the cowshed) to the studio, keeps its old shape intact. In the background, 'Sacco' chairs by Zanotta.

Another view of the living room. The metal bookcases are suspended from the wall, as is the blue-coloured radiator. Spotlights attached to two metal bars give an illusion of lowering the ceiling. The metal supports of the chairs are painted white and tend to disappear into the background of the white floor. At the end to the left, on a ledge of the door, a parrot-cage. On the back wall, Daniel Buren's

Conceptual work tracing in strips of different coloured paper the idea of an arch where a real one should have been. On the opposite wall (see previous pages) there is a paler version using wallpaper turned the wrong way round.

The kitchen and dining room connected by a wide, flattened arch and actually forming one large room, a sort of second living room. No cupboards; everything in sight, hung from the rack over the stove or placed on shelves. The oval table came with the farmhouse. The

dresser is 17th century from northern Italy and has at some time had its surface specially treated to resist the cold. Multiples by Andy Warhol, and Plia seats by Anonima Castelli round the oval table when there are guests.

INDUSTRIAL STYLE CONDOMINIUM

A linotype works erected in the printing district of Chicago in 1886 has recently been converted by Schroeder and Associates into modern loft-style apartments. This has inevitably meant a great deal of adaptation, but – except for the addition of new bay windows on the south side – the brick exterior has been left virtually unchanged. Inside, as well, the bare brick walls have been kept as they were, together with the original beams and most of the old rough floors. However, complete blocks of 'interior architecture' to accommodate the services – and sometimes sleeping areas – have been inserted into the living units, and these have a style very much their own. So don't be surprised if what looks at first sight to be a baroque temple turns out to be a highly modern kitchen. Schroeder and Associates are practised experts at putting rooms into rooms and framing their constructions in columns and pediments which are often a formal reply to a purely structural problem. In this case, the formality is not overwhelming because the architectural blocks are the only fixed element. The rest of the space in each apartment flows freely, and you can do with it just what you will.

Far left: the front of the Mergenthaler
Building, the old linotype works, showing the
new bay windows of glass and red-painted
metal. The skeleton of Tom's Grill has been
deliberately left as an example of an 'urban
ruin'. Before long, ivy will grow up it and
give the idea a more apparent validity. Top
left: the architects have profited from the
height of certain rooms to put in a new
mezzanine floor (generally accommodating the
sleeping area) and have clothed the upright
girders in fake Doric columns made of wood.
Bottom left: a sitting area has been placed
lower then the rest of the floor and completely
tiled. The imposing architrave and fake
columns resolve a real structural problem with
theatrical panache. Above: brightly painted
central heating ducts and – framed in one
window – the Sears Tower (highest skyscraper
in the world, designed by Skidmore Owings
and Merrill and completed in 1974). Above
right: in another apartment, a tabernacle
kitchen incorporating central heating piping
and turning it into a decorative element. In
front of the counter, 1930/40s bar stools.
Above: a 19th-century table, and two classic
Mies van der Rohe seats produced by Knoll
International. Bottom right: an 'unbuilt'
section, relaxation mattress in the centre.

THE PLACE where we decide to take up residence cannot always be put back simply as it was in its days of glory and then furnished according to the latest fashionable whim. Often our needs do not coincide with those of the people who lived there before. So rooms have to be reshaped, walls have to be knocked down, other walls have to be erected, floors have to be repaved ... In short, the place has to be reconstructed and, if this is to be done properly, it requires much sensitivity in reconciling new and old, in giving due measure both to the present and to the past.

Owner: Aldo Businaro Photographer: Aldo Ballo

RECONSTRUCTION

A HOUSE
REBUILT FROM MEMORY

In November 1974, the Superstudio in Florence received a letter from Germany asking if they could undertake the conversion of a building comprising a pharmacy, a doctor's consulting rooms and two apartments. This was followed

in January 1976 by another letter confirming the first, and in April there arrived drawings on millimetre-squared paper elaborating on the original proposal. The plans – which included a circular staircase emerging unexpectedly from one outside corner – had a poetic precision which persuaded the Florentine partnership to translate them into practical architecture involving no more disturbance to the existing pattern than was absolutely necessary.

The correspondent was Rainer Krause, a young pharmacist with a passion for design, and the building was a little late 19th-century brick house with a pointed roof in Lübeck. The general idea was to conserve the outline of the old house, which stood at an angle of 45° from the street, but to superimpose another at an angle of 90°; and this has now been done. The new building is basically a cube topped by a horizontal cylinder, while the lines of the old structure appear as positive and negative triangular prisms. The walls following the new line are all clad in square grey ceramic tiles: the glazed angles that correspond with the old shape are decorated with bands of blue-grey mosaic. Blue-grey is also the colour adopted for all the wood casings. Lead has been used as a covering for the curved surface and the two ends of the cylinder that crowns the roof.

The interior of the pharmacy on the ground floor is all in grey with endless rows of drawers and containers with their handles, relieved by

a Man Ray mirror; and with glass and ceramic vessels – including some incredible Sottsass and Vistosi specimens – decorated in uniform lettering.

The upper floors are reached by an entrance leading directly from the street. The hall and staircase have a transparent ceiling and a silvered pillar that seems to be supporting a slice of sky. After the consulting rooms on the upper floor, one comes to the penthouse, which is like a conservatory with all those windows framed in blue-grey – except that not all plants would take kindly to the leaden vault over those diagonal walls or to the illumination at night provided by Superstudio's alabaster lamps.

From outside, the semi-cylindrical penthouse (flanked by two roof-terraces and covered with leaden slabs held in place by copper hooks) looks like an upturned boat – or maybe a capsized ark.

Each façade of the house is different from the other. A unifying element is supplied, however, by the jutting-out and indented corners of the old outline with their fascias of sky-grey mosaic.

Far left: the principal façade overlooking the street. Above: the back elevation facing the garden. Wall cladding is in grey ceramic tiles with edging of blue-grey mosaic at the corners. Wooden casings are painted in blue-grey as well. The semi-cylindrical roof has a covering of lead. Left: a view of the pharmacy.

Opposite above: the living room in the penthouse with the window overlooking the garden in the form of a triangular prism. Driade chairs and a Zanotta table. Alabaster lamps are by the Superstudio. Opposite below: in the porthole room, on a console table, four little models of houses by Adolfo Natalini, with the corresponding drawings on the wall. Left: another view of the four sculptures. The first is of a house drawn when Natalini was five years old, the second is of a Greek urn in the form of a house copied from a schoolbook, the third is of a house designed at a time when Natalini was deeply committed to architecture, and the fourth is of this very house done at a time when he was thinking of giving up architecture. Above left: a view of the penthouse from the roof-terrace. Above right: a view showing the staircase with the steel chimney and accessible flat glass roof.

CONCRETE AND IRON
IN A PALLADIAN SETTING

The Palazzo Bonin Longare in Vicenza boasts an illustrious past, having been completed at the end of the 16th century under the care of Vincenzo Scamozzi. Today it is split up into well-appointed middle-class apartments, and one of these – on the top floor where the guest rooms once were – has been converted by Flavio Albanese (in collaboration with the architect Piero Morselletto), for the use of a young couple, in tune with Albanese's notions of 'functional rejuvenation'. What this meant in practice was removing the accretions of various epochs – partitions, false ceilings and so on – and then redistributing the original space to bring it into line with modern needs, creating an intermediate floor and certain walls (or half-walls) with membranes of ferro-concrete, while at the same time avoiding an effect of rigid subdivision. The new building elements – ferro-concrete, white-painted iron beams, etc. – make no attempt to compromise the old structure, being instantly recognizable for what they are. And the largely open plan doesn't seem too austere, perhaps because ribs of stone let into the parquet floor tactfully sketch in where the different rooms are intended to be.

Top left: the façade of the Palazzo showing its double order of columns and, above, the row of square windows looking from the reconstructed apartment. Right: the apartment front door in concrete and painted iron. Far right: the way through the living room from the entrance to the rest of the apartment.

Above: the living room with B&B Italia sofas and a double-fronted fireplace in violet-painted metal framed in curved concrete wings. Right above: another view of the living room *showing a half-wall supporting the staircase leading to the mezzanine floor. Right below: the dining room with a great table of walnut and rosewood designed by Albanese.*

REDISCOVERING A HERMITAGE

A 15th-century cottage sandwiched between two new 'pavilions' looks down through its old windows on to a large living room transforming the space into a stage courtyard, the kind of courtyard typical of building layouts in the Veneto countryside.

We are in fact at Arcugnano on the crown of Monte di San Fise in the Berici hills south of Vicenza – a geographical position which implies that the owner has chosen a certain way of life: solitary, far from the city, self-sufficient as on an island. And it was the need for self-sufficiency that the architect Federico Motterle – who designed the house for himself and his family – had first in mind when he began by deciding the best spot for siting the cellar where all the cheeses and preserved meats would be stored and the bread baked.

The general plan of the house is very simple, taking as its points of reference the original cottage (preserved intact) together with a great wall placed behind it and overlooking the valley. Round these two elements the new rooms were planned, or rather the different

pavilions disposed. These have direct connections between the outside and the upper floor and, although not symmetrically aligned, form a 'fascia' which with the great perimeter wall encloses the exterior space at the rear. The perimeter wall also acts as a sort of hypothetical porchway, especially in summer when the glass doors opposite are open.

Particular attention has been given to the choice of materials. Soft stone from the Berici hills predominates, but there are certain structures of reinforced concrete. Traditional materials and old decorating methods have been revived in finishing the interior walls.

The 15th-century cottage, restored and modernized, and now sandwiched between two newly constructed wings.

Above: the large living room – a sort of covered courtyard – overlooked by a bedroom corridor on the left side and by the original building on the right. The upper floors of the complex traverse the stage courtyard by means of footbridges, and the photograph has been taken from this level. The tapestry on the left-hand wall is Brazilian. Right: the dining area with a hearth intended not only for a fire but for quiet relaxation. The curved architrave is made of local stone in dovetailed blocks, and there is a small window in the shape of an eye. Far right: the outdoor eating area protected by a massive stone wall. Of the same stone is the dining table – poised almost like a springboard over the valley below.

Overleaf left: the stage courtyard, taken from ground level. Right: Guest area with a mezzanine studio erected in the centre of the room and reached by a steep flight of staggered steps.

Carlo Scarpa (1906–78) has rightly been called a poet-architect, and his language – invented word by word – has had a profound influence elsewhere; its vocabulary has been recorded and played back to the point of becoming part of a more widely shared experience, an idiom that others can employ in search of artistic excellence. But that is the fate of all good poetry. And Carlo Scarpa knew he could always create new poetry from new experience, because his work always arose from an accurate study of data, case by case. There is no one solution that applies to two different problems or two different places; nor are there ever two identical problems.

For this reason the 'Professor' was reluctant to design 'ready-made' buildings; and for this reason he loved things that had been cherished by human hands, things that had a direct corporeal link with the creative process. He loved the gestural quality, the simplicity and the nobility of traditional materials, with their secret associations and the old-fashioned methods of working them, into which he had a supreme insight. In the same individual spirit, he planned not only buildings, interiors and gardens but also the manner of viewing them, of looking at them in their right dimension, their right perspective. It was not by chance that he became a master of restoring and redesigning museums or preparing important exhibitions. And nothing was left to chance in his work, either. On the contrary, everything was bound together by the simplest (and therefore the most ineluctable and convincing) logic. People were aroused to look and look again; as happens with a great painting which we first take in as a whole, then examine closer to analyze the brush-strokes, the material, the technique, the mixture and blend of colours and so on – and then step back from in order to derive a more complete, informed and profound satisfaction.

The meticulous care given by Carlo Scarpa to detail (first in design and then in ensuring perfect workmanship) required considerable time, effort and patience, not only from the author but also on the part of his clients; and that is one of the reasons why only a few of Scarpa's private houses ever got much further than the drawing-board.

One that did – the Villa Zentner in Zürich – was constructed on the foundations of an older house, a neo-rococo confection of 1914; and local planning regulations placed certain limitations on the new building's size. In practice, this meant that the back elevation facing the garden could be extended but the front building line – and the width – had to be retained. The façade was, however, completely changed. While certain openings were kept in their original positions, the whole house was mounted in a slim setting of bronze outlining the corners and window-frames. The simplicity of exposed cement was consciously exploited but the plainness was relieved by insertions of green, gold and silver Venetian glass mosaic, which give a first taste of the magisterial matchings of colours and materials which so richly pervade the interior.

The choice of furniture, objects and pictures, apart from the large drinks cabinet and the dining table (progenitor of the famous 'Doge' model produced by Simon International), has been left to the practised taste of the owners.

Above: the garden elevation of the Villa Zentner built on the foundations of an older house. The inlays of green, gold and silver Venetian mosaic enrich the simplicity of the exposed cement.

A VILLA REBUILT BY CARLO SCARPA

The upper living room with ceiling and walls in glossy Venetian stucco and a floor in two different kinds of wood. Pictures by Victor Vasarely, Max Ernst and Antonio Tapiés. Two Jacob chairs.

Above: a view taken from the dining room's internal balcony, which one can see also in the photograph below projecting out into the lower living room. Above right: the dining room with its great central table of marble, ebony and rosewood on a base of bronze. The table top decoration is an inlay by Carlo Scarpa of various precious minerals – old Greek marble, porphyry, green serpentine and Spanish fire marble. To leave the table unencumbered, the chairs – except at mealtimes – are turned towards the side counters. Right: the large 'walk-in' drinks cabinet with the door open.

AN EARLY
CORBUSIER HOUSE

'When I designed this house I was called Jeanneret,' wrote Le Corbusier in a letter of thanks to the architects who had refurbished it in the late 1950s after it had lain for years in a state of neglect. At the time it was built – between 1914 and 1916 – Le Corbusier was indeed known as Charles-Edouard Jeanneret, not having yet adopted his celebrated pseudonym.

So Le Corbusier doesn't repudiate this villa put up in a small Swiss village, even if he assigns it to a very remote phase in his career, to a sort of juvenile limbo, when he was still under neo-classical influences, before having embraced *le sentiment moderne*. On the contrary, he mentions it in his book *Vers une Architecture*, citing it as an example of how the geometrical relationship between measurements determines the monumentality of a façade.

Inside, the sense of space is overwhelming: there is a very high hall open at the sides to two semicircular rooms and two rectangular recesses; a curving balcony looks down from above; a huge window bathes the whole scene in a flood of light.

The architects entrusted with the work of restoration and furnishing (Angelo Mangiarotti and Bruno Morassuti first, then more recently Mangiarotti in collaboration with Chiara Pampo) took on a fairly formidable task. First and foremost, they had to eliminate all the arbitrary additions that had been made over a period of time and return the structure to its original state, as Le Corbusier had first envisaged it. Then they had to select contents that would not compete with the building but have an integral rapport with its style. For the central area they chose very low pieces, barely off the ground, so as to enhance the room's vertical thrust. In the semicircular rooms at each side they were careful to plan round the horizontal axis.

A good collection of modern French paintings has been incorporated, but they have been hung here and there with deliberate casualness to avoid the appearance of a museum.

Below: the front of the villa overlooking the street. Right: a detail of the garden side showing the large window that spans two floors.

Top left: from the upper storey balcony which leads to the bedrooms, a glimpse of the semicircular living room/library. To the right, a sculpture by Jean Dubuffet. Top centre: a view from the floor of the hall illustrating the connection with the flanking rooms.

Right: seen from the dining room, the hall and the other semicircular room opposite. Chandelier of Murano glass hooks by Mangiarotti for Vistosi.

The central hall seen from the large window. The furniture pieces have been kept very low to accentuate the room's exceptional volume. On the walnut and granite table in the foreground, a work by the Spanish sculptor, Eduardo Juantegui Chillida.

Right: the big living room which has been planned on several levels. Left: another view of the living room and its large geometrical windows. Vibieffe sofa.

AN APARTMENT
IN THE SKY

Architect Bruno Sacchi has taken a rather nondescript one-floor house – a typical bungalow put up during the first quarter of this century, in a seaside town on the Ligurian coast – and by ingenious reconstruction has turned it into a remarkable building with greatly increased habitable space. The old four-pitched tiled roof with its bulky substructure of wood has been removed and replaced with a light copper covering supported only by four iron rafters bolted together at the apex and connected to tie-beams running along the outside walls. As a result, the previously wasted area in the roof can now be put to good use; but the most striking feature is the extra illumination provided by ribbons of glazing which split each supporting rafter into two. A great expanse of irregularly shaped glass, facing the terrace that looks towards the sea, also lets in much needed light. The internal floor arrangement has been completely changed with levels cleverly staggered to produce cunning dimensional juxtapositions, emphasized by the colours of the new pillars and girders, which are painted sometimes blue, sometimes orange, sometimes white. Two identical fireplaces, one above the other on different floors, add to the new vertical emphasis.

The fireplace on the upper level which is
identical with the one below. Windows of
various shapes as well as the ribbons of light
from the roof throw into relief the tremendous
diversity of the wall surfaces – even though
these have been uniformly finished in white
Genoese stucco. Floors are in slabs of
travertine with a 'carpet' of Emilian
terracotta. Right: two arched French windows
opening on to the garden. The raised sitting
area has Vibieffe sofas and a little bookcase
under the porthole.

RESTORATION, if anything, surpasses even re-construction in its demands on sensitivity. Faced with a building designed by a famous name, or laden with past associations, the restorer obviously has to proceed with the greatest caution and respect. We offer here a few examples of buildings that have been reinstated with particularly pleasing results. These range all the way from a Palladian villa in the Veneto to a group of structures clustering higgledy-piggledy round a tower in Tuscany. Due obeisance has been made to historical precedent, but the rest-orers have concentrated on creating a sympathetic ambience in which most of us would be very happy to live.

Architects: Machado & Silvetti Photographer: Studio Azzurro

RESTORATION

THE SMILE OF THE MALCONTENTA

Built on the banks of the Brenta Canal so as to be within easy boat distance of Venice, the Malcontenta (or Villa Foscari), after painstaking restoration carried out a few years ago, now appears as Palladio conceived and created it around 1558 (and subsequently described it in his *Quattro libri dell'architettura*), commissioned by the noble Foscari family who had owned land in the district since the 12th century.

The villa is in the form of a cube, with the addition of a great Ionic portico on the side looking towards the canal, and has a classic, noble simplicity. There is a congruity of proportion both in the scansion of the differing external surfaces and in the arrangement of the interior spaces, symmetrically distributed and subdivided according to Palladio's theories which envisaged for each room a set ratio between height, length and breadth – a logic of spatial relationships founded on the laws of musical harmony. Despite this mathematical precision, however, the building retains an enigmatic and mysteriously allusive quality – as indecipherable as the Gioconda smile. Therein may lie its chief fascination.

Legend has it that the original 'Malcontenta' was a young woman of the Foscari family who was shut up in the villa as a punishment for improper conduct. But the name is really attached to the district and probably refers to the waters of the Brenta being *mal contenute* (badly controlled), or to the humour of the local populace, exasperated at having to suffer perpetual floods. Whatever the derivation of its name, the Malcontenta continued in the ownership of the Foscaris until the end of the 18th century. Then, with the fall of the Venetian Republic, it participated in Venice's general decline. During the siege of Venice, it was a billet for Austrian troops; and in World War I, it was a military hospital. Later still, a granary.

So the villa was sadly reduced in circumstances when acquired in 1926 by the rich and cosmopolitan Bertie Landsberg, and it was thanks to this benefactor that the structure was saved from complete devastation. The uncovering of frescoes that had lain hidden under several coats of whitewash, the restoration of staircases, balustrades and columns – these were just some of the works undertaken. By his own account, Landsberg kept the

Top: a magnificent pronaos embellishes the façade of the villa looking towards the navigable Brenta Canal. Centre: the two-storeyed central hall. Frescoes are by Gian Battista Zelotti with scenes depicting the Metamorphoses of Ovid. Bottom: the lower floor entrance from the garden. Venetian theatre statues in wood of Armida and Rinaldo. Opposite: a room frescoed with grotesque figures.

furnishing simple to conform with the dignity of the rooms; and this spirit of discretion has been fully respected by the present owners, who are the Foscaris – finally returned to their old property. Antonio Foscari, who now lives in this ancestral home with his family, happens to be a keen architect; and it was he who directed the most recent restoration of the exterior, patiently resuscitating old skills and locating the few artisans still able and willing to practise them.

Top: the dining room with old convent store-cupboards and a 16th-century sideboard along the walls. Traditional Veneto pottery as well as some pieces by Fratte Rosa. Centre: the kitchen with its typically 16th-century layout. Bottom: a bathroom with a tub of pink Verona stone. Opposite: a bedroom called the 'Bacchus Room' because of the vine-covered pergola in the fresco.

A NEW LIFE FOR AN OLD CASTLE

This ancient towered farmhouse, or castle, or fortified villa, which goes back to the 14th century and stands proudly in the Roman countryside, needed four years of patient and sensitive restoration under the care of Piero Pinto to transform it into a suitable home and atelier for the well-known fashion designer Laura Biagiotti.

It would be almost an understatement to say that the building had come down in the world since the 15th century, when it was occupied and largely given its present form by the nobleman Marco Simone. But when Laura Biagiotti saw it she fell for it on sight; and since that *coup-de-foudre* in 1977 it has been a love story all the way – *and* one with a happy ending.

Not that there weren't many difficulties in between. 'At the start', says Piero Pinto, 'we found ourselves confronted by a ruin, full of charm but still a ruin. The first thing we had to do was to decide where to begin and what should be our guiding principles – what to preserve and what to sacrifice. Where to put in toilets and bathrooms and things without destroying the ambience.' But the task was rather larger than that would imply. Later superimpositions to the structure had to be removed; all parts of the building had to be assigned their new functions, and for this, connecting links were all important. The stairways, in particular, presented a problem. To reach the upper floor there was an outside staircase, and it was only after the work of restoration was at an advanced stage that Pinto – following a hunch and taking a chance on undermining the tower – found internal stairs which had been filled in with earth.

Pinto's plan was to take this gaunt relic of a house and domesticate it while preserving – even enhancing – its historical associations.

As for materials, those of local origin have been favoured wherever possible, including salvaged tiles and bricks, terracotta, travertine, 'Roman stucco' (powdered marble, chalk, cement and clay bound together by a method that goes back to Pompeian times) and white ceramic tiles with a translucent quality for Pinto's speciality: floors made to look like carpets. Here and there, simple and consciously ingenuous decorations have been used – such as patterns applied by rollers or stencils

Top: a front view of the towered farmhouse associated with Marco Simone, also known as the Villa Cesia. On the upper floor left can be seen the arch of the 15th-century gallery reopened during the work of restoration. The great tower dates from the 14th century. Centre: a room in the tower with a Thonet chaise-longue. Bottom: a corner of the kitchen showing how new tiles can create a striking yet traditional effect. Opposite: an entrance from the internal courtyard leading to the 'White Drawing Room'. Herring-bone paving with old bricks; metal-framed glass door.

Above: a view of the drawing room. This had been cut up into three little rooms, but has now been restored to its original shape, with the 16th-century frescoes uncovered. On the floor, rectangles of travertine let into the terracotta conserve a memory of the three small rooms. The statue in the centre is 18th century, school of Rome. Right: the principal bedroom, with white silk curtaining the walls

which were once the country substitute for wallpaper.

Furniture is in a mixture of styles, as you might find in any old country house. Some items look as though they had always been there – and that's a crucial test. In fact everything has been put together to create a carefully casual impression. Nothing looms.

So here is the happy ending of a love story involving all sorts of people: Laura Biagiotti, Piero Pinto and many others. For Laura there is also the satisfaction of having discovered and helped save a far from negligible piece of artistic heritage. To have befriended a building of such remote birth and such enduring merit – and to have given it such an assured future – is no mean achievement for someone used to working in the transient world of fashion.

and the canopy of the Viennese four-poster made of cherrywood and bronze (1830). The Agrippina couch of 1840 is also upholstered in *white. Bottom: a bathroom, with a 19th-century onyx shell, probably originally a fountain, serving as wash basin.*

A CASTLE FOR ALL SEASONS

This early 14th-century castle in the Lombardy countryside, not far from the gates of Milan, once belonged to the Visconti and, as part of a vast agricultural estate, was an administrative centre as well as a source of military protection. Then, in 1357, Gian Galeazzo Visconti donated it to Bianca of Savoy; upon her death in 1380, it went to the Clarissas of Pavia. And so it became a convent – and later a boarding-school.

When the present owners (a Milanese couple) acquired it in 1974, it was completely abandoned – more or less a ruin. Their intention was to make it their principal home (with a small apartment in the city serving as a pied-à-terre for foggy evenings) and they engaged architect Alberto Mazzoni to undertake the restoration. The work was extremely laborious but was carried out with due regard for economy, and in the end the expenditure involved compared favourably with the cost of a property in one of the exclusive modern developments that are going up all the time around Milan.

Courtyard and kitchen are the parts of the castle that seem to give most consistent pleasure throughout the year. The courtyard with its portico and gallery – and its profusion of flowers – offers the sort of protection that makes it seem like an outdoor living room.

The building's harmonious internal structure has been preserved; features such as doors and vaulted wooden ceilings have – where necessary – been carefully reinstated. Furniture is of all types, mostly family pieces from previous homes. Objects, too, are a happy accumulation of memories – of domestic life and foreign travel.

Top left: the west front, remodelled with large windows during the 17th century. The turret on the right was added for purposes of defence. Bottom left: the 14th-century tower which is the earliest part of the castle and which originally stood alone, circled by a moat, dominating the surrounding countryside. The high ogival arch is a relic of the old drawbridge. The stone bridge crossing the moat was built at the time the new entrance was made. Right: the internal courtyard with its portico and gallery – and the principal tower peering over the roof.

Top: another view of the courtyard taken from the gallery. The paving has been done with old stones unearthed during the work of restoration. Bottom: the portico, much used for relaxing and outdoor meals.

The kitchen with 17th-century sideboard and 19th-century table used for dining. With the stove so near at hand, guests don't have to be deprived of the cook's conversation.

FROM THE
13TH CENTURY
TO TODAY

On the left-hand side of the Arno, in the countryside near Florence, there have been catalogued some seventy surviving houses erected by the middle classes during the economic boom enjoyed by that city during the years running roughly from 1250 to 1330. Known as *case da signore* ('gentlemen's houses'), these constructions typically take the form of low buildings, usually of stone, clustering about a central tower, which predates them and round which they grew up over a period of time.

One such *casa da signore* has now been lovingly restored by the architect Bruno Sacchi as a home for himself and family, with studio attached. On the ground floor a series of rooms leads naturally into one other, culminating in the spacious living room, with its open fireplace and a great expanse of glass which looks through archways on to the paved interior courtyard. But the most interesting aspect of the conversion is up above. Not one of the new floors (replacing the previous ones that had rotted) cuts into the old stone walls.

Only the essential girders holding and supporting the floors have contact; the floors themselves are clearly detached, and all round there runs a chink of space which lets through light and reveals the continuity of the stone structure. Not even stairs touch the precious stonework, being simple ramps attached to the floors. Where it has been possible to uncover them, traces of 14th-century decorations can be seen here and there. These consist of repeated stencilled motifs and one or two coats of arms, for example of the Peruzzi family who once owned the tower.

Above far left: the medieval courtyard seen through the old portico which has now been glassed in and turned into a living room. Left: the living room looks on to the courtyard through a virtually continuous expanse of glass which runs along the arches but a little way behind, so as to preserve the illusion of still being in the open air. From outside, the window-frames are invisible. Below left: the dining room with a great trestle table. Two scaffolding holes made when the tower was built have been opened up and provide additional light. The ceiling has oak beams with planks of chestnut, and the walls still bear traces of the stencilled 14th-century decorations which are stylized depictions of ermine skins. Below: the children's room – a sort of house within a house on the top floor of the tower.

WHAT KIND OF setting should you give to a work of art? Is it easy to live with a few prized pictures and pieces of sculpture? Or with an entire collection? The examples presented in this chapter (villas or city apartments of artists, collectors and gallery owners) demonstrate how you can make room in your home for a few collector's items or even play host to a very wide and comprehensive range of works. In each instance, a love of art has brought with it character and charm. Houses have not been turned into mere exhibition centres, nor has the presence of so many striking objects eclipsed the personality of the owners.

Architect: Nanda Vigo Photographer: Aldo Ballo

LIVING WITH ART

AN IVORY TOWER

To accommodate a large part of his modern art collection, the painter and connoisseur Remo Brindisi commissioned architect Nanda Vigo to build him a villa at the Lido di Spina (Province of Ferrara) by the seashore. Completed in 1972, it stands behind long white conventional walls: a distinctive structure of compact proportions. The windows are few and far between and are of minor importance since the interior illumination has been devised principally to show off Brindisi's acquisitions. A diffused light (natural by day and artificial at night) shines down from the ceiling of the central cylindrical space, which is wide as a small piazza and tall as a tower (12 m in diameter and 12 m high). All the interior surfaces are lined – and patterned – with tiles of white clinker, carefully placed to obtain interstices of a consistent 1 cm width. Alternate panels of satined and mirrored glass transmit and reflect light along the curved sides. The helicoidal staircase is strongly outlined by the solid, sinuous steel handrail. At the bottom of the stairwell, a circle of black-upholstered sofas on a circular black carpet seems like an island where you can land to chat or meditate, surrounded on every hand by a white sea of applied and fine art.

Above: the building as seen from the street. Nanda Vigo's architecture achieves an impressive monumentality by the subtle manipulation of simple shapes: note the striking effects of light and shade produced by the cantilevered terraces. Right: a large mural by Lucio Fontana. Underneath the mural, a sculpture by Giò Pomodoro and other small works.

Above: the helicoidal staircase which curls round the tower's internal walls, as seen from above. The sculpture at the bottom of the stairwell is by Carmelo Capello; the Perspex trees are by Marotta. Alternating panels of satined and mirrored glass filling the

apertures which give on to the surrounding areas are by Nanda Vigo. The wall and floor tiles are of white clinker. Top right: a room of trapezial proportions with furniture by Magistretti for Artemide. Pictures are by Giacomo Balla, Umberto Boccioni, Henri

Matisse, Jackson Pollock, Virgilio Guidi, Gino Severini, Wols, Giorgio de Chirico, Alberto Savinio. In the next room, you can just see a Chagall and a Magritte. Centre right: the entrance hall with the start of the staircase. Beside the first steps, two slim

figures by Alberto Giacometti invite you to begin your ascent. Below right: another Giacometti, with its reflection, in a niche between the dining and living rooms.

147

Top left: a mirror-framed bed and a work by Emilio Isgrò created expressly for this room. Centre left: a sitting room on the second floor. Pictures by Brindisi, Balla, Franz Kline and others. Bottom left: the dining room dominated by a large work of Brindisi's. Windows screened by looking-glass. Above: the taverna for eating in a hurry, or in a crowd. The glass shelves against mirrored backgrounds hold many small pieces of sculpture.

Above: the entrance hall to Michelangelo Pistoletto's flat in Turin with his mirror-picture of 1962/63, Holy Conversation. Anselmo, Zorio and Penone; *also his* Burnt Rose *of 1966 in painted and burnt corrugated cardboard. His statue* The Giant *of 1981 stands like a monument in the centre of a piazza.*

MIRRORS AND ILLUSIONS

'At times', says Michelangelo Pistoletto, 'I've wondered which would be the ideal city to live in and I've never been able to make up my mind. All I know is that now I couldn't live anywhere but Turin.' So this noted conceptual artist, born at Biella and brought up in Turin, after sampling a succession of habitats including Berlin and six different cities in the United States, has finally come back to his true love.

When he returned with his family, he took a rather dark apartment with wallpaper and flower patterns everywhere, and his first step was to paint everything white. The second step was to move out contents so as to allow space for his pictures and sculptures. Now entire rooms are devoted to his works, which are nicely set off by their dazzling white backgrounds. With the furniture having been so drastically thinned out, there remain just two or three rooms where one can sit and eat or watch television. The theme running through the whole apartment is that of a looking-glass. It begins in the hall, when one finds oneself faced with two corridors leading in opposite directions, and continues with Pistoletto's famous mirror-pictures hung on the walls. Two dining rooms, very similar but not exactly alike, intensify the slight feeling of intellectual vertigo conveyed by the pictures. But the looking-glass effect reaches its apotheosis with the artist's two daughters. Moving lightly and silently through the rooms, they seem – with their identical clothes and hairstyles – to be reflecting each other. They are twins.

Overleaf: a room containing Pistoletto's Venus of the Rags, *1967, and – on the right –* In the Sphere of Cloth, *1980. In the corridor, a mirror-picture of 1973,* Naked Woman with Red Gloves.

Right: the television room with Pistoletto's picture Ti Amo *and a bench of his design in wood and marble.*

THE HOUSE OF WONDERS

Alexandre Iolas's holiday home – all white marble – is set among olive trees in the stony hills where sprawling, chaotic Athens finally peters out into the surrounding countryside. Rose bushes line the driveway; orange trees grow in the patio, also paved in white Greek marble. But, besides being a holiday place, this is a private temple of art – Surrealist, Pop, Metaphysical, classical, neo-classical and so on – not art embalmed as in a museum but art free to impart its own vitality to others.

Behind this phenomenon lies a process of slow accumulation, motivated by a lovable, capricious obstinacy and an absolute devotion to beauty wherever it may be found. Furniture, objects, works of art, books, flowers have all been chosen and grouped with shrewd and masterly self-confidence by this sympathetic sorcerer of our time, who is perpetually in flight between his various art galleries in the capital cities spread out over the globe.

Over and above his role as a dealer, Iolas

has been a friend to almost all the great contemporary artists – Giorgio de Chirico, Matta Echaurren, Max Ernst, Takis, René Magritte, Salvador Dalí, Juan Miró and Andy Warhol, to name but some – and it was he who introduced the Surrealists to the United States at a stage when a Max Ernst or a Magritte could be picked up for little more than $500 apiece.

Coming from a Greek family resident in Egypt, Iolas travelled the world before decid-ing to put down roots in the country of his ancestors. It is there that he now finds an opportunity to relax in his brief respites from business activities. It is there, too, that he has created a magic house where a blue period Picasso can converse intimately with an an-cient marble head, the two-and-a-half millen-nia separating them being easily bridged through the alchemy of this redoubtable connoisseur.

Left: a corner of the patio with a sculpture by Takis. Below: another view of the house – built for Iolas by the Greek architect Pikionis – showing the front porch and, to the right, an Attic stela of a young man with arm raised in greeting. At the foot of the columns are pieces of 11th-century sculpture from Ravenna (Aries is Iolas's zodiacal sign). Below right: one of the guest room French doors looks on to a part of the garden which harbours a bronze figure by Magritte, Le Therapeute.

Above: the entrance hall with a pink Brauner of 1959 over a settee by Lalanne. Top: also by Lalanne is the copper and brass balustrade to the staircase. At the foot of the staircase stands a Magritte boot (1967). Beside the door, a 3rd-century Greek relief featuring a cornucopia of good luck. Left: a tranquil corner of the studio/music room with a Magritte of 1962, L'Ovation, a small classical marble, and a sculpture by Brauner of 1945, Tot-in-Tot. Flowers have been placed in a Roman silver chalice. Right: the dining room, with two oval 'spatial concepts' by Lucio Fontana, and two Picassos over the console table. Louis XIV silver chandeliers and on the table two French candelabras with crystal and topaz pendants in the likeness of pears, apples and lemons.

Right: a corner of the room devoted to canvases by Brauner and pieces of Egyptian art. The Brauner work shown here, entitled Rêverie, is placed between a black granite head of the 12th Dynasty (right) and a funeral mask on top of a column. On a boule cabinet – inlaid with tortoise shell, mother-of-pearl and coral – are other precious Egyptian pieces, including a wooden head of the 19th Dynasty. The rug is Tibetan. Below: Iolas's private room with a huge picture and tapestry, both by Matta, dated 1968 and 1951 respectively. Sculptures in the corners of the room are also by Matta, as are the couches cut out in free shapes like pieces of a puzzle from polyurethane and produced by Gavina-Knoll. On the 18th-century table of pink Verona marble, candlesticks with moths burning their wings in the flames by Dali. Spheres are by Takis; so too is the little bronze on the right placed on a stool-sculpture by Finotti. The 17th-century baroque spiral columns are in pink Verona marble. Opposite: in the foreground a 'sardine tin' bed by Lalanne (a soft sculpture in satin); also by Lalanne, the rocking-bird. The calibrated metal shaft is by Alain Reynaud and the phallic monument is by Man Ray.

A SALON FOR THE IDENTITÉ ITALIENNE

In an apartment on the third floor of a palazzo in the Piazza San Carlo, Turin, where Vittorio Alfieri wrote his early tragedies, Christian Stein has both her home and her gallery. 'I wanted to show', she says, 'that work is my *raison d'être* and my life is inseparable from it.' As a gallery owner she has important achievements to her credit in promoting *Arte Povera*,

which has developed into a movement whose exponents are almost all Turinese by birth or adoption and which Paris has recently labelled as *L'Identité Italienne*. But even more than a dealer, Christian Stein is a private collector, and things in her personal possession – works of art, valuable furniture pieces and objects of different periods, all chosen with great indi-

viduality of judgment – rub shoulders with the gallery exhibits. The latter are naturally always changing, but at times – as with a show of Mario Merz, which coincided with our visit – spill over from the canvas on to the walls and doors and floors and become almost indistinguishable from the furnishings belonging to the apartment itself.

Above: the entrance hall to Christian Stein's gallery taken during the Mario Merz exhibition and showing one of his works. Right: one of the rooms, with a white-painted

Biedermeier cane sofa and a row of classically simple upholstered couches. The 1920s style chromed metal tables are from a design by Eileen Gray. Below right: the billiard room

where the great 1925 table is echoed in the Merz picture on the wall with cue made out of neon strip. 'Primo novecento' chairs and a typical 1930s dressing-table.

Left: an entire room is taken up by Merz's long, winding table of iron, glass and granite. The chairs are copied from a Bauhaus pattern. Bottom left: the bathroom furnished with 1930s furniture pieces painted white, and pottery of the same period. Bottom right: a corner of the study with a 1920s tallboy. Opposite: another view of the study with an 18th-century chair drawn up behind the desk. Sculpture by Paolini, and in the foreground a modern chair taken from a 1920s model by Eileen Gray.

Possessing an avant-garde art collection can determine the physiognomy no less than the atmosphere of an apartment, such as this one situated right in the centre of the old quarter in Milan. The occupants are a young family who have installed just a few pieces of furniture and a selection of what in dealers' jargon are called 'environmental objects', i.e. conceptual or minimalist works. To accommodate these as well as some sculptures and pictures, the planners of the Studio Castelli decided on a setting that would be uniform and neutral, in no way intrusive: walls and ceilings done in gloss white, floors of tropical wood or covered in overall carpets of powder-blue. Masonry half-walls separate the dining, living and entrance areas without breaking up the interior, as would happen with conventional walls. Most of the furnishing is modern, but there are also a few antique pieces to provide a good-natured contrast with the items of contemporary art.

Left: the living room. Surrounded by Gae Aulenti sofas, a 'carpet sculpture' by Carl Andre (1965) with a chequerboard pattern composed of steel and magnesium alloy tiles. To the right, Luciano Fabro's Piedone *in glass and shantung. Going further back, a mobile by Alexander Calder and a female figure by Rod Dudley. On the left-hand side, an oil painting by Mario Schifano and, against the half-wall shielding the dining area, two triangles in wood and polyethylene by Carla Accardi. Above: in the study next to the dining area, an effect of disorientation is produced by Gaetano Pesce's out-of-scale Naska-Loris lamp-sculpture. A Frank Stella painting takes up the whole back wall. Writing-desk by Superstudio for Zanotta.*

Overleaf: the dining area with art déco table and chairs in briarwood and mother-of-pearl by Dufrène. On the floor, another carpet sculpture by Carl Andre, this time in copper and lead. On the right, a minimal work in galvanized sheet iron by Donald Judd (1965). On the left-hand wall, a work of the 1960s by Jannis Kounellis. The four mirrored cubes are by Robert Morris. Coloured glass vases are by Sottsass for Artemide. The neon tube sculpture is by Dan Flavin. In the passage leading to the entrance is a work by Jim Dine.

CREATIVITY is a modern religion with many converts. There are people – notably fashion and show business people – who in the name of imagination and creativity are constantly fostering and killing off new myths (while often erecting vast economic empires on the remains). So it is only natural that the ferment should spread to lifestyles and that the homes of many involved in art, fashion or some aspect of the visual image should be in perennial transformation, perpetual flux. These people rarely splurge too much on furnishings because tomorrow there may be a new look and everything will have to be thrown out. What we are seeing is a shifting, transitory world in which values become strangely disembodied.

LIVING WITH IMAGINATION

CHANGING INVENTIONS

In a house built in 1924 on Wilshire Boulevard, Los Angeles (reputedly by the newspaper baron William Randolph Hearst for the actress Marion Davies) live two artists: April Greiman and Jayme Odgers. They also work there and with the pompous Hearstian decor have reached their own *modus vivendi*, answering back to it with impudent effects produced by modifying things of little material worth – effects that can change according to the mood of the day. The day we called the mood was dominated by a dark red sunset with black clouds over the ocean, so it seemed only right that they should be spray-painting a chair a deep shade of cyclamen and making a light fitting in an 'exciting shape' out of lemon-yellow paper. April refers to these enterprises as 'different games'.

Different games, various tools, common objects bought from motor accessory supermarkets, things costing only a few dollars – these create a sense of cheerful anarchy in what would otherwise be a distinctly sombre ambience.

Chairs in the sitting room, draped in quick-change shrouds of coloured cloth, seem like judges interrogating somebody accused in absentia, *while the blank face of the cooking-foil mirror confirms there is indeed no one there.*

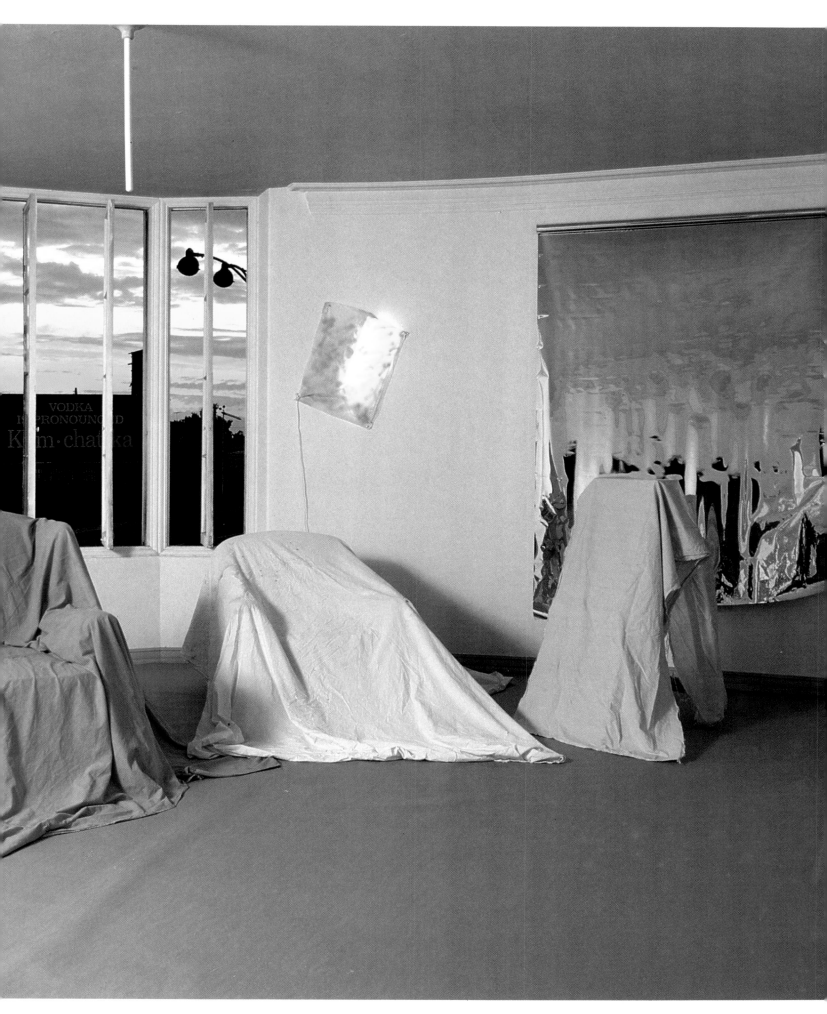

Above: light fittings in 'exciting shapes' which can be changed according to the mood of the moment. Top right: in a niche in the entrance hall, two floor mops crossed like heraldic halberds. Bottom right: no fire in the fireplace – just the cold presence of a globe and a mirror. Opposite: in the hall passage, with its original 1924 carvings carried out by skilled Mexican craftsmen, another lamp (this time in a palais-de-dance gown) and a luminous goose bid the guests welcome.

POP TROMPE L'OEIL

Zandra Rhodes, the gifted fashion creator, often changes the look of her London house, and this was a version which reflected perfectly the mood of the late 1960s: extravagant use of paint, brightly coloured fabrics, paper flowers like Christmas decorations – a sort of cross between Surrealism and Pop. Anyone who has studied Rhodes's work over the years will be able to see connections between this interior and her fabric and fashion designs. Specially representative of the period are the kitsch objects picked up in forays through London's open-air markets and the large mural done by the Australian Martin Sharp which adds an imaginary dimension to the physical space confined within four walls.

On the wall beside the staircase which leads to the upper floor is a huge mural in bright pop style by Martin Sharp, influenced by the artistic experiments of the 1960s.

Opposite: the decorated doorway and the small table with its tea setting are examples of the fanciful details which have gone into the heterogeneous style in which the home is decorated.

A HOME IN A GARAGE

It is probably because of his work as a photographer that Uwe Ommer is so responsive to the stimulus of changes in taste. At a time when in Italy only trendsetters such as the fashion creator Walter Albini seemed to have picked up the message from across the Atlantic, Ommer was among the first in Paris to do over his apartment in the style of High Tech. Earlier still, when the Pop influence on fashion and interior design was shading into the 1950s revival, Ommer – and this was ten years before Jean Jacques Beineix's successful film *Diva*, whose leading character lives in a kind of garage – transformed his 145 m² third-

floor apartment in the Faubourg St-Antoine into a sort of 'mo-pad', with a nice metalled blue 1950s Chevrolet bought from a breaker's yard forming the *pièce de résistance*. Under the bonnet he installed a drinks refrigerator, and in place of the seats a snug double bed: the boot served as a storage trunk. This multi-purpose totem set the tone for the rest of the flat, with the walls done in creamy white corrugated iron and the floor – also white – given an outdoor surface. The sole objects of decoration were a Coca-Cola placard, a parking meter sculpture, a luminous plastic tube (Ommer's own design – and this too ten years ahead of its time,

becoming a decade later an item of mass production), and a picture by Don Eddy show-ing – in continuation of the central theme – a car being demolished. Ever in the vanguard – in fact, years before the celebrated interior decorator Andrée Putman turned it into the fashionable trick it now is – Uwe Ommer was covering the table and the old armchairs and sofas in the living area with white sheets, as if for a conference of ghosts, or as if the owners of the house were permanently away on their summer holiday. The light in the living space is shielded by a road sign which lets us know that the whole thing is really just a mishap.

The mo-pad in Paris done up in the Pop idiom and with more than a whiff of exhaust fumes about the decorations and the recycled contents. Top left: the bathroom with a Coca-Cola placard, a round sunken bath and casually placed mirrors. Bottom left: worn-out sofas and table have been covered in starched sheets and lit with ghostly effect by a single electric bulb hidden behind a road sign. Below: the garage bedroom with a Chevrolet bed, a parking meter and strips of paper covering the window in imitation of a garage door. On the ground there is a luminous tube.

FORMS AND SYMBOLS

This Paris flat belonging to the gallery owner Yves Lambert doesn't betray its previous incarnation as a workshop. Andrée Putman, who converted it and could – had she wished – have turned it into an open plan loft, has chosen instead to make it into a conventional apartment with clearly demarcated rooms. Now the walls are strictly white and the ordinary wooden parquet floors have been painted in a dark shade of grey. So far, nothing exceptional. But then, disorientation creeps in. The apartment's main furniture pieces – the sofa in

the living room and the ottoman in the bedroom – have had their functions put in doubt. They've been transformed into fleeting and ghostly presences with cloth coverings that conjure up visions of mediumistic ectoplasm. For reassurance one has to cling to the plaster columns, fresh off some set, standing around like film extras with a lightweight nonchalance that – paradoxically – makes you realize they have their feet planted very firmly on the ground.

*Above: dustsheets envelop an anonymous
sectional sofa arranged round a low glass and
marble table ('Metafora' by Vignelli). Above
right: the bedroom with two plaster columns
and a plain ottoman covered in a marble-
pattern fabric by Mira X. Below right: the
bathroom with two mirrored doors. On the
vanity unit, an archaeological find.*

PROVISIONAL ROOMS

Architect Laurids Ortner, of the Austrian group Haus-Rucker, has a profound aversion for the sedentary, settled way of living and subscribes neither to the traditional concept of the house as private property nor to the modern movement idea of the home as a provider of shelter and safety, packaged in unornamented containers. Instead, he regards today's man as a nomadic animal and talks of 'temporary architecture', which he has put into practice in this apartment. The rooms are half empty and such pieces of furniture as there are have a primarily formal significance. As for elements of architecture, there are four white pillars, looking rather lost (as though they had strayed in from a service station or a bus shelter or from the entrance to some bathing establishment) and intended to act as psychological room dividers. Two of the pillars are topped by a curved architrave making a kind of doorway that separates the dining and living areas to a greater or lesser degree, according to how the Venetian blind hanging from the architrave is disposed.

Right: the large dining table with seats of various shapes and sizes, like a scene from a Biedermeier restaurant. Opposite: the Venetian blind has been lowered. Also, a bar (backed by a settee) has been pushed into place, intensifying the restaurant effect. Note the fittings casually attached to the pillars.

HAD YOU EVER thought of contriving a window curtain with fresh flowers scattered between two sheets of cellophane? Or building yourself a small domestic theatre? Or devising a smaller house inside a bigger one that resembles a transparent shell? Or making yourself a sort of stage apartment where the scene can change rapidly from one act to the next? These are just a few bright ideas – some very simple, others complex and costly – that we have gathered here and there from the pages of *Casa Vogue*. But everyone's home can be a source of ideas. You only have to learn how to seize them and develop them in your own way.

IDEAS FROM CASA VOGUE

CURTAIN CALLS

It is often said that great inventions spring up spontaneously, at the same time, in different parts of the world.

Knowing the floral themes of Ken Scott's printed fabrics, we were prepared when visiting his Milan apartment for the incredible hanging garden in the courtyard outside, but were slightly caught off balance by the remarkable curtain of fresh flowers in the window.

Meanwhile, in a San Francisco apartment wittily decorated by William Passarelli, another of our correspondents found that the art dealer Joseph Tornabene had screened his old iron bathtub with a transparent plastic shower-curtain containing biros, felt-pens, coloured pencils and pastels.

Left: the flowered window looking on to the hanging garden and illuminating Ken Scott's drawing-board and bedroom. The idea of decorating a cellophane curtain with fresh flowers 'in the manner of Ken Scott' came from the fashion designer Cinzia Ruggeri. Below: the San Francisco bath curtain has so many pockets as to be almost a storage unit. Here it contains pens and pencils but it could also hold toothbrushes, toothpaste, toilet soap, aftershave and a million other things.

ONE ROOM WITH LOTS OF ELBOWROOM

Two young designers, Margherita Del Favero and Alessandra Parma, have shown how to live in a single-room apartment, with a kitchen in one corner, and still enjoy a feeling of space.

The kitchen, triangular in shape, is screened from the rest of the interior by a wooden partition and three sliding panels, which transform it into a kind of domestic theatre where the cooking and washing-up can be played out as a daily drama. The *trompe l'oeil* pictures on the panels give a depth of field, a sense of scope. Elsewhere in the apartment, an absence of small furniture pieces contributes to the same feeling of free movement.

The two designers and the painter of the panels have all been inspired by the 15th- and 16th-century paintings of Giovanni Bellini, Piero della Francesca and Andrea Mantegna, to whom they have turned for their use of false perspective, their sense of chiaroscuro and their palette of colours – not to mention the Renaissance 'divine proportion'. A thoroughly contemporary solution to the needs of modern living thus has its roots in Italian artistic traditions going back hundreds of years.

Above: the kitchen with the sliding panels closed. Right: the kitchen with the sliding doors open. The ladder goes up to a storage space behind the false skylight.

A HOUSE WITHIN A HOUSE

When the Prague architect Borek Sipek set about planning a house to be put up in a Hamburg suburb, he was required to observe the local regulations which prescribed rows of virtually uniform structures with sloping roofs and built 6 m one from the other on plots only 14 m wide. This he duly did, and the authorities obtained their house with a sloping roof and of the desired volume – but only in name, because the official house is a skeleton of steel and glass. The real house is of stone placed diagonally inside this transparent envelope, with just two corners peeping cheekily out at the back. In time, a little winter-garden will grow up between the inner and outer walls. Meanwhile, this system of integral double-glazing has already demonstrated its worth in the form of delightfully modest heating bills.

Top left: the principal façade with the entrance lobby showing the inner front door set at an angle of 45°. Bottom left: the living room/roof terrace covered by the outer roof of glass. Chairs in metal tubing and rubber by Alias. Right: two pictures taken at night and illustrating more clearly the relationship between the glass and stone structures.

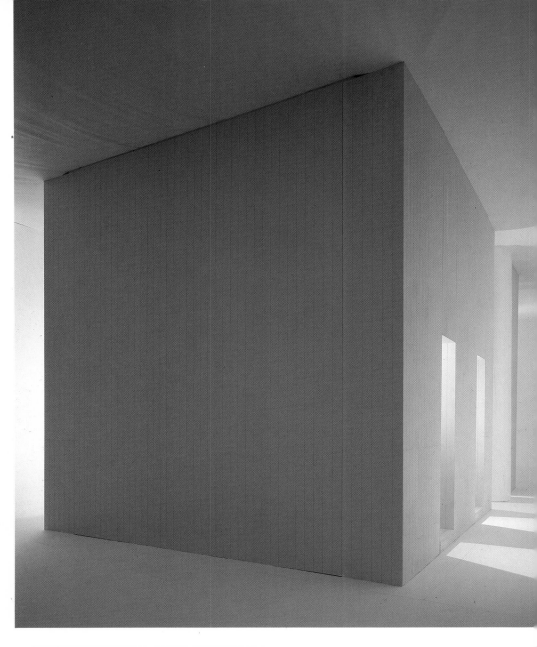

A THEATRE AT HOME

Aldo Rossi has always been intrigued by the theatre and has undertaken many projects connected with it, including the Teatro at Parma, the 'Teatrino Scientifico', the Teatro Carlo Felice di Genova (reconstruction) and – perhaps most fascinating of all – the ephemeral 'Teatro del Mondo' floating on the waters of the Venetian lagoon.

Shown here is his first practical domestic theatre, intended to be placed bodily in a much larger room such as a loft or a gymnasium, like a game of Chinese boxes. This particular model – with its piece of stage sculpture representing a monument done by Rossi for his cemetery at Modena – was designed for a commercial exhibition; but the architect is already thinking of other, more permanent, applications for the idea.

Top right: from the outside, Aldo Rossi's domestic theatre looks like nothing more than a simple wooden cube. Bottom right: the stage with a small model in red recalling one of Rossi's most renowned works, a monument designed for his cemetery at Modena. Opposite: from the entrance a side view of the stage and a glimpse of the auditorium. Seats produced by Molteni.

ARRANGEMENT FOR OUTDOOR MEALS

We are in the hills of the Veneto, the same hills that were so loved by Petrarch who spent much time there at Arquà. Here may be seen various *palazzetti*, not grandiose villas put up by the local nobility, nor farmhouses, but something in between: buildings probably erected by rich merchants some time in the 17th century. One of these was restored with the help of Carlo Scarpa, who took a special interest in the design of the threshing-floor and the part of the garden set aside for eating out-of-doors.

Below: the threshing-floor has been paved in bricks and cement and inclined towards two discs representing the sun and the moon. This piece of pagan symbolism was inspired by certain old frescoes discovered inside the palazzetto. Left: two views of the alfresco eating place with its great corner chimney and decorations of inlaid Murano glass. There is a brick floor. The structure is of exposed concrete. The beams and trelliswork overhead are of iron. Behind the chimney there is a pool with aquatic plants, as in oriental gardens, so one can dine to the cool plash of water.

LIVING WITH BLUE

Not only is the house cobalt blue, but so too are the fountains and pools in the garden. The pergolas are turquoise and the balustrades green. Cement paths are pink and bordered in azure, as are the flower beds. The building's door and window frames are done in sunshine yellow. A pretty daring colour scheme even now, one would say, and even more so in the 1920s when the French painter Jacques Majorelle (son of the famous furniture maker Louis Majorelle) left Nancy in France to come and live in Marrakech, making the blue house his home. Its architectural style has a unique charm, combining as it does rationalist ideas with traditional Arab elements such as the jutting-out portico. The garden was created over a period of forty years and is one of the most incredible to be seen anywhere, mixing blue and green – the colours of love and peace – to give an effect that is immensely relaxing and cheerful at one and the same time. Now a public park, it borders on to the Marrakech property of Yves St. Laurent, who – together with his right-hand man Pierre Bergé – has assumed the task of restoring the little pleasure-house and its grounds.

Two views of the building where Jacques Majorelle lived from 1922 until his death in 1962. After 1962 the garden was more or less abandoned until its recent rescue. In front of the house is a large pool.

Left: a close-up view of the house. Below: various glimpses of the garden where many species flourish – palms, succulent plants, agaves, bougainvillea, philodendrons, papyrus, caladium.

SOME HOUSES are like milestones. They symbolize and sum up an entire cultural era, a current of taste, an expressive mood – and not just in architecture. These houses fit a certain moment as exactly as a fruit fits into its own skin; and for years they have remained unaltered, bearing miraculous witness to a former climate of ideas, to another way of living, to circumstances that can never be recalled. They may be houses with principles to proclaim; or houses which offer us a detailed portrait of the person or persons who lived there. The examples shown in our final section represent perhaps the most important and lasting part of what I personally consider to be the best of *Casa Vogue*.

DOCUMENTARY HOUSES

THE 'MAISON DE VERRE' (1920s)

Pierre Chareau's glass house in the Rue Saint-Guillaume, Paris, is one of the most unchallenged architectural works of our century. More than that, it is positively venerated and has been taken up and cited by admirers ranging from neo-rationalists to post-modernists simply because its masterly, ambiguous complexity enables it to be read in so many different ways. In fact it has now become a cult with its own fan club: Friends of the 'Maison de Verre'! But when *Casa Vogue* first featured it in 1971, not many people had heard of it, and only a few pictures had been published of it – notably in an American university magazine.

A contributory reason for the present enthusiasm is undoubtedly that it is one of the

comparatively few houses typifying a period to have survived for over fifty years *exactly* as conceived by its creator. But that is not to detract from its intrinsic merits. As Francis Jourdain has pointed out, Chareau was an architect in everything he did. His invention was never applied to 'decorating' a house. He was always concerned with its function in meeting both the material *and* spiritual needs of the person who was going to occupy it.

The person in this case was Dr Jean Dalsace, an exceptional client, who has explained how 'thanks to an old lady who didn't want to leave her crumbling apartment on the second floor, Pierre Chareau had to bring off a real *tour de force*'. What he had to do was to carve three well-lit storeys out of the old ground floor and upper floor of a little *hôtel particulier* which were previously being used as offices and were so dark that the employees worked all day with the lights on. This Chareau did brilliantly. Overcoming enormous difficulties owing to the complexity of the layout – with interpenetrating rooms, some of which were on two floors – he succeeded in devising a unique piece of architecture accommodating consulting rooms on the ground floor and a private apartment in the two storeys above. The materials utilized for the construction were spartan: metal and concrete-framed glass. Despite this, however, the house has about it an air of great wealth: a wealth of light – in all its variations throughout the day – and a wealth of space.

Below left: the 'Maison de Verre' seen from the main entrance. Right: the great wall of concrete-framed glass lit up at night.

Right: the great hall seen from the second floor gallery. Sofa and screen are by Lurçat. Note the bookshelves running the whole height of the two floors.
Below: a general view of the main bedroom, and a detail showing a briarwood chest of drawers produced by Chareau in 1918.

A HOUSE
IN THE WOODS
(1930s)

At Noormarkku, Finland, in 1939, Alvar Aalto – the northern master of 'organic architecture' – built a house in the woods for a couple of friends who were patrons of art and receptive to his ideas. The house was conceived on an open plan, with large windows, and was intended to have a close empathy with its outdoor environment. In the event, a happy partnership of author and clients resulted in an emblematic piece of contemporary architecture in which Aalto's talents were revealed to the full.

For the inside, a rich variety of materials was used. These consisted mostly of wood, but there were also black-painted steel pillars – standing singly or grouped, covered to differing heights in wicker-work – which symbolize the surrounding forest's invasion. The slim poles placed irregularly beside the staircase are meant to represent the trunks of saplings.

Aside from its subtle and sensitive articulation of space and mass, every detail of the house has been thought out with ingenuity and love – just look at the rhythmic effect created by the ceiling joists – and this partly explains how Aalto's concept has been translated with such resounding success into practical form. As he himself said, the architect should harmonize the world of matter with the life of man.

Below: the huge picture window looking out from the entrance hall of Villa Mairea to the trees. The ceiling has been lined in wood. Top right: a view of the exterior, showing the overhanging balcony shaded at one point by a roof-canopy. Exposed surfaces have been partially clad in wood. Bottom right: another aspect of the house, this time reflected in water.

Left: a detail of the big living room with a group of two steel columns faced to a certain height in wicker-work. The wall panels are removable to cater for all occasions. Below: the piano veneered in briarwood with curved steel legs and a glass top. Right: a corner of the living room looking towards the entrance hall from which it is separated by a low wall and a series of poles in polished wood. The lamps have been specially designed.

Above: the verandah with traditional wicker-work armchairs plus a low table and trolley, both designed by Aalto and still in production. On the table, a horse by Marino Marini. In the background, the usual removable partition – note the corrugated upper part, a feature of other walls. The spherical lamp hanging in the centre is traditional Finnish. Opposite, top left: another shot of the living room looking towards the

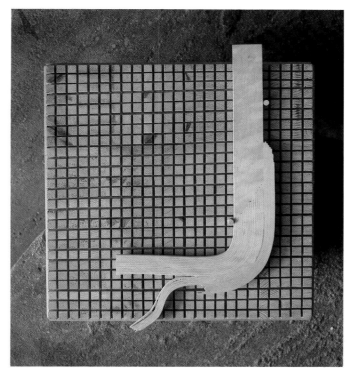

entrance, with an old Finnish copper vase in the foreground and behind a standard lamp by Alvar Aalto with the stem and base covered in black leather and the diffuser made of white-painted metal layers (still in production: Artek). Top right: a panel sculpture by Aalto in wedges and layers of wood. In the small photographs: two details with a flower vase designed by Alvar Aalto. Below right: a view of the large fireplace.

THE RESTLESS IMAGINATION OF CARLO MOLLINO (1940s)

'A work is always a stroke of imagination,' wrote Carlo Mollino to Gio Ponti in the 1940s. And he always stayed true to that maxim when producing works for the Turinese middle classes – a stratum of Italian society with profoundly European traditions, even if hidden under a veil of shyness and provincialism.

Casa Vogue published photographs of this interior, created in 1943/44, in April 1974. That was some time prior to the general rediscovery and re-evaluation of Mollino, and certainly before the full force of the 1940s and 1950s revival. Now, in his own country, Carlo Mollino is thought of rather as the Italian Alvar Aalto and is widely appreciated as one of the most brilliant designers of his period. (A curious thing about him was that he was ambidextrous and could draw with great speed and precision using both hands at the same time.)

His schemes, whether for buildings or furniture, are distinguished by a sort of pent-up energy, like a spring about to be released. His forms are dynamic and modelled in the likeness of animals and even human beings. Quite often his seats, armchairs, mirrors – even his architecture – recall animate entities as diverse as a woman's body, a gazelle, or insects such as a locust or a cricket. Because of his naturalistic morphology and his sense of spatial flow, he

Left: the dining room with a piece of Lucio Fontana pottery set in the centre of the superb table. Along the wall are a series of three-legged chairs looking like car seats, and above them a shelf with panels of mirrored glass.

has often been bracketed with followers of the Scandinavian 'organic' movement. But he differed from them in possessing a greater charge of vitality, a higher degree of expressive force.

Right: the living room seen from the raised level of the dining room. Note the chimney suspended from the ceiling. At the end on the right, a photographic enlargement of an old print which forms the background to an oval picture by Fontana. The bookshelves behind the chimney are partly shut off by sliding glass panels. The storage unit in the foreground (with sculptures by Sofo and Teshihara) is in the shape of an asymmetrical spindle and can be rotated on its one foot. This and the three-panelled door with diagonal bars are typical of their period.

A ROUNDHOUSE
AT UDINE (1950s)

This villa, built by Carlo Scarpa during the second half of the 1950s (and finished in 1960) for the Veritti family at Udine, is full of architectural surprises. It also has the distinction of being one of the few residential projects which Scarpa brought to fruition overseeing every last detail himself.

Clearly inspired by the 'organic architecture' of Frank Lloyd Wright, it is based on a circular plan with a framework of imposing cement pillars and with a front that is glazed the whole height by large windows divided from top to bottom by broad bands of wood. Both vertically and horizontally, the house has a spatial fluidity and dynamism – with sudden *deus ex machina* interruptions – that are the product of an extremely subtle and complex design.

Important use has been made of built-in furniture which plays a key part in organizing the interior space. As would be expected, materials were selected with loving care, and everything was done to achieve a high quality of workmanship. There is an expressive eloquence in every particular and a felicitous choice of colours throughout. In short, there are present all the elements which – added to Scarpa's formidable building skills – have contributed to this architect's well-earned fame.

Opposite far left: the front of the house looking towards the gate. Above left: a detail of one of the pillars which look like giant totem poles and form the framework of the building. These are made of prefabricated cement sections moulded to designs by Carlo Scarpa and creating various vertical patterns according to the order in which they are laid. The pillars also have lights at the top. Opposite below: the south front looking over a pool. The great expanse of glass which runs the whole height has a timber frame of Douglas fir. On this page: two views of the conservatory contained within the tall exterior windows and the inner wall which bounds the living room below and the master bedroom above. The glass fixture shutting off the living room was added later. The bedroom window can be closed by means of sliding panels finished in stucco.

Left: a picture that gives some idea of the very complex interior arrangement. Through doorways, windows and skylights you can see from one small passageway (left) the dining room sheltering under the protective wing of a green false ceiling, or (straight ahead) the living room and entrance hall, or (above) the corridor connecting the bedrooms, or (below) the basement tavernetta. In the wall at the back of the dining room can be seen the door

leading into the kitchen lobby and an old-fashioned serving hatch. Centre: the staircase from the entrance hall to the first floor with mahogany panelling and stairs. In the background on the left, the living room. In the foreground, one of the totem pillars with a fitted light at ceiling level. Right: one of the pillars seen through a glass skylight from the cellar. Built-in furniture is of mahogany and spruce.

Top: the master bedroom has sliding panels at the window and, at the head of the bed, more movable panels opening on to the upstairs sitting room. The door at the far end can be opened to its full height or, if preferred, just at the part that has been painted. Bottom: the kitchen lobby with all furnishings specially designed. Right: the stairway seen from the upper floor. The walls have been finished in a variety of materials (mahogany, cement bricks, Venetian stucco and rough plaster) and these combined with the different shelves and windows go to make up a rich and subtle decorative scheme in their own right.

A HOUSE OF GOTHIC TALES

The manor house shown on these pages is the place where Baroness Blixen (pen name Isak Dinesen) was born, spent the greater part of her life, died and was buried. Now it is occupied by the Danish Academy and Karen Blixen's old housekeeper – and, of course, the ghosts of the author's *Gothic Tales*. Indeed, the building – situated halfway between Copenhagen and the Castle of Elsinore, on the Danish coastline facing Sweden – looks ready to give birth to a tale of its own, in the fashion of an

Isak Dinesen story that contains within itself the plots of many others.

Having been brought up here, Karen Blixen returned in 1931 after a long period spent running a coffee plantation in Kenya. She had been finally defeated by drought and the world slump in commodity prices. So she came back to Rungstedlund, where her mother and other relations were still living, settling down in her brother's old room and in her father's old study, working at the desk where her father

(also a traveller and writer) had produced his books a generation before. 'First things first' was one of her favourite sayings, and for thirteen years she never unpacked the things she had brought back. The only exception was a painted wooden screen that had stood near her fireplace in Africa. This she wanted to have close to her so that the mythical African and Oriental episodes depicted on its surface should continue to be part of her everyday reality.

Left: Rungstedlund (situated near the town of Rungsted in Denmark), surrounded by meadows and woods and bordering a small lake. Top centre: the two windows that look out from Karen Blixen's old bedroom. The room below was her study. Bottom centre: a side of the house that faces a large meadow. Right: the verandah with black and white squares painted over stout wooden floorboards.

Top far left: the drawing room, known as the green room. Note the white curtains of embroidered tulle that spill on to the floor.
Bottom far left: Karen Blixen's study, simply – but not austerely – furnished. On the desk inherited from her father, there is still the little portable machine on which the author typed every word of her writings. Above and below left: Karen Blixen's bedroom with its old iron stove and timbered walls.
Immediately below: African shields and spears hanging on the study wall over a bookcase and next to one of the several original iron stoves that the author collected from other Danish and Norwegian country houses.

REFERENCES AND CREDITS

The picture stories in this book appeared originally in CASA VOGUE as follows:

INDEX